Thomas EDISON

FOR KIDS

His Life and Ideas

LAURIE CARLSON

21 Activities

CHICAGO REVIEW PRESS

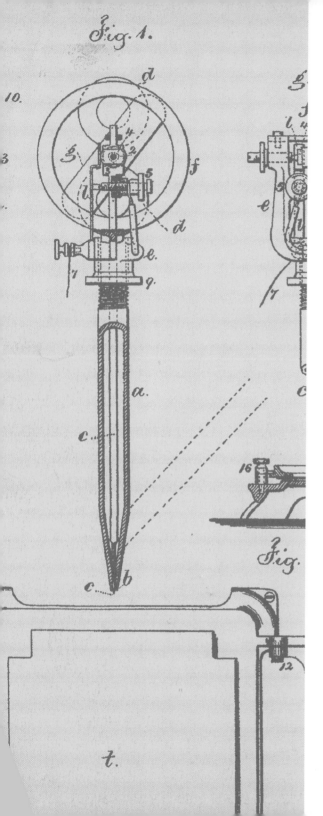

Library of Congress Cataloging-in-Publication Data

Carlson, Laurie M., 1952–
    Thomas Edison for kids : his life and ideas : 21 activities / Laurie
Carlson.— 1st ed.
        p. cm.
    Includes bibliographical references and index.
    ISBN 1-55652-584-2
    1. Edison, Thomas A. (Thomas Alva), 1847–1931—Juvenile
literature. 2. Inventors—United States—Biography—Juvenile literature.
3. Science—Experiments—Juvenile literature. I. Title.
    T40.E25C37 2006
    621.3092—dc22

                                                        2005025659

"Make a Steam-Powered Boat" activity adapted with
permission from *Gonzo Gizmos* by Simon Quellen Field.

Cover and interior design: Monica Baziuk
Interior illustrations: Laura D'Argo

Published by Chicago Review Press, Incorporated
814 North Franklin Street
Chicago, Illinois 60610

ISBN-13: 978-1-55652-584-1
ISBN-10: 1-55652-584-2

Printed in Italy

5   4   3   2

FOR BRIAN, WHOSE ENTHUSIASM GOT ME INTERESTED IN THE GREAT MAN
IN THE FIRST PLACE, AND FOR TYLER, WHO HELPED WORK OUT THE
EXPERIMENTS AND ACTIVITIES. YOU BOTH REMIND ME OF THOMAS EDISON.

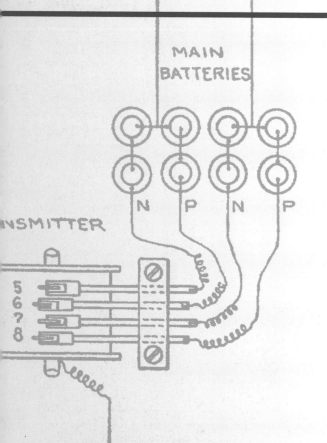

Contents

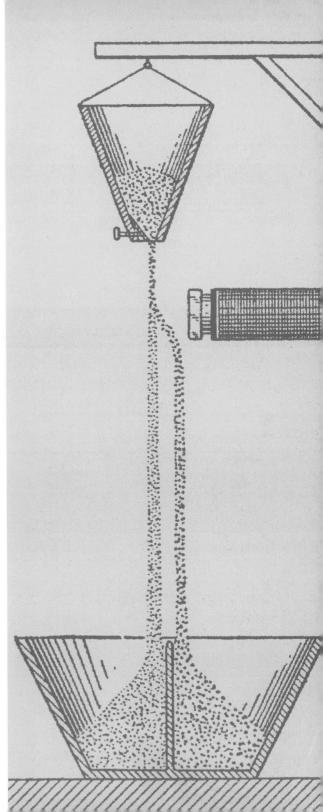

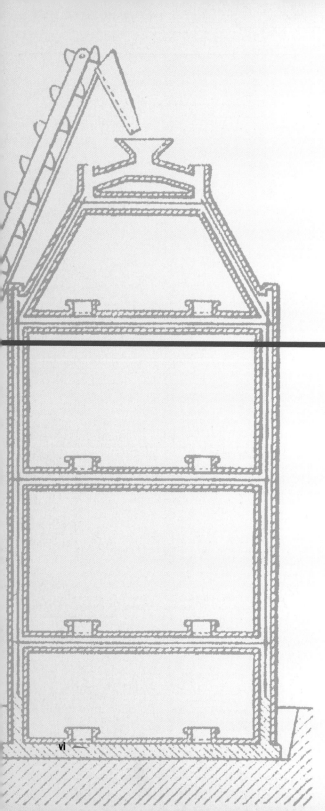

Note to Readers

What's in a Name?

THOMAS EDISON went by a variety of names at different times in his life. His parents named him Thomas Alva Edison but called him Al as a boy. When he went off to New York to begin his inventing career, he used the business name Thomas A. Edison. As an adult, his friends and family called him Tom. When he became famous, people referred to him simply as Edison or by such terms as "the Wizard." This book will use the names most commonly used by Edison himself: during his childhood, he went by Al; as an adult, he used Thomas. Don't let the changing names confuse you. We're always talking about Thomas Alva Edison.

Acknowledgments

I HAVE LOTS of appreciation for Cynthia Sherry and Curt and Linda Matthews at Chicago Review Press. Every project we've done together has been a joy. I can't thank them enough for being great people to work with. Many thanks also to Lisa Reardon, editor, who has been attentive to detail and a pleasure to work with.

My thanks for research, archive, and photograph help extends to several people, especially Jean-Paul Agnard, Edison Phonograph Museum, Quebec, Canada; David Burgevin, National Museum of American History, Photo Services; Paul Israel, Thomas A. Edison Papers, Rutgers University, Piscataway, New Jersey; Kathy Hoke, Ohio Historical Society; Laurence J. Russell, Edison Birthplace Museum, Milan, Ohio; Victoria B. Scott, Edison National Historic Site; Hal Wallace, National Museum of American History, Electricity Collections; Edward Wirth, Edison National Historic Site.

Thanks to Ed Carlson for reading the manuscript and for finding the rusty old phonograph—I never would have known what it once was! And, of course, thanks to Tyler Carlson and Brian Bruegeman for their ideas and help with the projects.

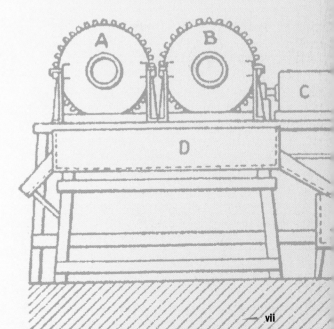

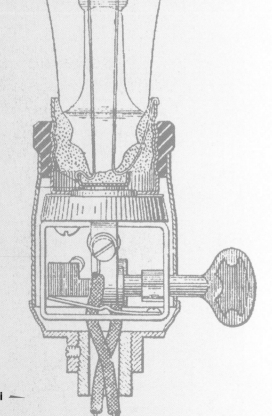

Introduction

THOMAS EDISON was one of the most important Americans in the nation's history. He was an inventor and a businessman, and his products and ideas made the world cleaner, safer, and easier to live in. Yet he never held public office, wrote a book, or taught a class. His parents were ordinary people, without much money, and he didn't spend much time in school. People often wonder why Edison was such a huge success.

As a child, he got into trouble a lot and seemed unable to learn (or so a teacher said). As a teenager, he drifted around, working as a telegrapher without earning much money or being able to settle down. When he made his first invention—the vote-counting machine—no one wanted it. Later in his inventing career, others sometimes copied and stole his ideas or sued him.

Some investors even pushed him out of his own company. He spent years in court and plenty of money protecting his rights as an inventor. He lost money on some projects, and at times couldn't pay his workers because he had not been paid himself. But he didn't give up.

So why did Edison succeed? How was he able to take simple ideas and make them into machines that played music, recorded voices, or flickered real life images on a wall? How did he become the most famous person of his day?

Thomas Edison was born at a time when technology was changing rapidly, when inventions were common, and when people were eagerly applying new advances in steam engines, telegraphy, photography, and electricity. Thomas Edison worked on inventions in nearly every field. He perfected many ideas that others had come up with, turning them into products that could be manufactured and distributed to everyone. His story is about the importance of learning, experimenting, and never giving up. It's about how an ordinary boy grew up to change the way everyone lived and worked for the rest of the century.

There are hundreds of books about Thomas Edison, yet no one book can tell all there is to know about him. He left crates of notebooks filled with ideas and reflections, as well as thousands of laboratory records. Hundreds of newspaper and magazine stories were written about him while he was alive. So many records exist that his papers have still not been completely studied by historians.

This book will describe what Thomas Edison's life was like, some of his inventions, and a few of his setbacks and successes. The activities will give you an idea of the scientific concepts Edison was exploring as he pushed his experiments on to success. Edison's success clearly began in his childhood. Many of Edison's inventions are rooted in the lessons from his schoolbooks and from experiments he did in his boyhood lab in the basement of the family home. His life was his work, and it began while he was young, studying what he saw around him and applying knowledge and effort to create things nobody had created before.

Time Line

1800 — Alessandro Volta produces electricity from a cell: first battery of zinc and copper plates invented

1814 — First practical steam locomotive constructed in England

1819 — Electromagnetism discovered by Hans Oersted in Denmark

1844 — Samuel Morse's telegraph used for the first time

1847 — Thomas Alva Edison is born on February 11 in Milan, Ohio

1854 — Edison family moves to Port Huron, Michigan

1859 — Thomas Alva Edison begins selling candy on the train running between Port Huron and Detroit, Michigan

1861 — U.S. Civil War begins

1863 — Edison works as a telegrapher

1868 — Edison patents his first invention: an electrical vote recorder

1869 — Edison goes to New York City Transcontinental railroad completed at Promontory, Utah

1870 — Edison invents a stock ticker machine and earns $40,000 for it. Begins an invention business.

1871 — Thomas Alva Edison marries Mary Stilwell on Christmas Day

1872 — Edison perfects the duplex telegraph Marion Edison born, the first child to Thomas Alva and Mary Edison

1876 — Edison builds a research laboratory at Menlo Park, New Jersey

Alexander Graham Bell invents the telephone; Western Union Company hires Edison to build commercial telephones

Thomas Edison Jr., the Edisons' second child, is born

1877 — Edison invents the phonograph

1878 — William Leslie Edison is born

x

1879 Edison invents the first practical incandescent lamp—the light bulb. It burns for more than 40 hours

1880 Edison discovers the "Edison Effect": the way electric waves move in space

1884 Mary Edison dies

1886 Thomas Edison marries Mina Miller

General Electric Company buys Edison stock, pushes Edison out

1888 Nikola Tesla invents the electric motor

Madeleine Edison is born, first child to Thomas Alva and Mina Edison

1889 First moving picture shown in the West Orange lab with sound coming from a phonograph record

1890 Charles Edison is born to Thomas Alva and Mina Edison

1893 Edison builds first motion picture studio

1894 Edison's first moving pictures shown in public

1895 Wilhelm Roentgen discovers x-rays

1896 Edison perfects the x-ray fluoroscope for surgery

1898 Theodore Edison is born

1903 Orville and Wilbur Wright successfully fly a powered airplane

1917 United States officially enters World War I

1926 Edison retires. His sons Charles and Theodore take over the Edison companies and laboratories.

1928 Edison receives a Congressional Medal of Honor

1929 Fiftieth anniversary of Edison's invention of the light bulb

Stock market crashes, Great Depression begins

1931 Thomas Edison dies on October 18

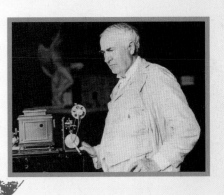

Birthplace of Thomas Alva Edison in Milan, Ohio.

> "WHAT SEEMS IMPOSSIBLE
> TODAY, MAY NOT BE TOMORROW."
> —THOMAS EDISON

Off to a Quick Start

Thomas Alva Edison's Boyhood

A TERRIFIC SNOWSTORM blanketed the small village of Milan, Ohio, the night before Thomas Alva Edison was born. It was 1847 and the Edison home, like others, was heated with a coal- or wood-burning stove or fireplace. Candlelight or the flickering flame from lamps lighted the darkness. Lamps were simple—a piece of wick stuck in whale oil or vegetable oil.

Dr. Lehman Galpin lived down the street from the Edison family and arrived to help with the baby's birth. He thought the newborn boy might have "brain fever" because the infant's head was larger than most newborns' usually are. It's hard to tell what he meant by brain fever, but his words struck fear in Nancy and Samuel Edison, who worried that their new baby might have health problems. Nancy had already borne seven children, but only three had lived. Those children were teenagers now, about to set out on their own. But the baby, named Thomas after an ancestor and Alva after Captain Alva Bradley, a Great Lakes ship owner and family friend, was a healthy newborn.

As a child, everyone called the boy Alva, or Al. His two sisters and a brother were much older, so Al spent a lot of time playing by himself. His parents had been married nearly 20 years when little Al was born, and they seldom played with him. Samuel Edison, Thomas's father, was born in Canada, where his father, John, had fled after the American Revolution. The older Edison was a Loyalist and refused to fight alongside the patriots. He remained loyal to Britain, but the British lost the war. The revolutionaries took his home and business, and he was forced to move his family to Canada after the war ended. When Samuel became an adult, he eventually moved to the Canadian side of the Great Lakes region, where he led a rebellion against the British government—this time he wasn't going to make his father's mistake. But the rebels failed, and Canadian government troops moved to arrest him, so he fled into the United States—the country his father had fled

from a generation earlier. Samuel and his wife Nancy settled in Milan, Ohio, a few miles from the southern shore of Lake Erie, where he earned a living selling lumber, roof shingles, and animal feed.

Though Al spent much time alone, he did have friends, and together they enjoyed swimming in the canal, building toy roads and wagons, and learning the songs of the lumber and canal workers.

When Al was young, Milan was a bustling trade center where farmers brought grain to be shipped out by canal to the Great Lakes and beyond. Most people were farmers in the early 1840s, and their crops were transported by oxcart. But new technology—canals—enabled the moving of products to market faster, on barges and steamboats. The Erie Canal in New York State was completed in 1824, allowing farm products and lumber to be shipped from places like Milan, Ohio, across the Great Lakes, down the Erie Canal, and to New York City. Long lines of wagons waited to load and unload their goods, and the Edison house was near the canal, right in the center of the action.

Al was like many children who strayed off into mischief, sometimes with scary consequences. He once fell into a nearby canal and

Thomas Alva Edison at 14 years of age. Everyone called him Al.

had to be rescued, his clothes dripping and his lungs coughing up water. Another time he fell into the pit of a tall grain elevator tank and was nearly smothered in the pile of wheat that closed over him. After secretly playing with fire in his father's barn, the wooden barn ignited and burned to the ground.

The barn fire not only destroyed the family's investment, as there was no fire insurance for such a catastrophe, but it threatened to burn the neighboring buildings, too. Fire departments in places like Milan were not equipped to save buildings, and neighbors were angry about the incident. Al's father held a public spanking of the boy (an acceptable punishment in those days), strapping him soundly in view of everyone.

Al's father loved him dearly, but often thought he was a stupid child. His father complained that the boy was always asking foolish questions and getting into trouble. Many of young Edison's problems came about because he was thinking about something else and not paying attention to what was happening around him. He and a friend had gone swimming in the creek one afternoon, and while Al sat on the bank, deep in thought, the friend drowned in the creek. Coming back to attention, Al figured the friend had already gone home, so he went home and said nothing. Later that evening the townspeople put out a search for the missing boy, his body turned up in the stream, and Al was blamed for the tragedy. His father thought Al was a miserable troublemaker, lacking good sense. Al started to believe it.

One fellow in Milan fascinated the young Edison boy. Sam Winchester owned a large flour mill powered by a steam engine, which was a new invention at that time. Machinery had previously been moved by waterpower or draft animals, but Winchester's steam engine used fuel to heat up water, which created steam to move the machinery. It was the age of the steam engine, and Al saw it firsthand. The steam engine was powerful, noisy, and hot, but Winchester had even more interesting projects going on at the mill. Townspeople called Winchester "The Mad Miller of Milan" because they thought he was crazy to be working on the foolish invention he kept in the mill. He was building a passenger airship. It was a large balloon powered by hydrogen that he hoped to fly someday.

Seven-year-old Al hung around the mill constantly. His father disapproved and repeatedly punished him for going there. But Al was fascinated by Winchester's dogged determination to build the airship, which unfortunately burned down the mill when some hydrogen ignited. Not one to give up, Winchester went back to working on the experiment and finally succeeded. It had taken several years, but Winchester went aloft, lifted up into the air by his balloon invention. He drifted slowly out over Lake Erie and was never seen again.

While the people of Milan weren't very enthusiastic about air travel, they were completely devoted to the idea of canal transportation. Their local canal had brought many opportunities to the area. They didn't like the idea of railroads, either. When railroad builders wanted to lay a rail line, the townspeople resisted. They didn't want a train to interfere with the shipping business they were doing on the canal. That was a big mistake, because in 1854, the Lake Shore Railroad built its rail lines elsewhere, and traffic shifted from the canal to the railroad. Farmers took their products to the newer and faster railroads, leaving Milan and its canal behind. In a few short years, the town was nearly dried up. There was little business, and people started leaving.

The Edisons sold their comfortable home for very little money and moved about 100 miles (160 km) away, looking for a better situation. Al was seven years old when the family moved to a rented house in Port Huron, Michigan, a thriving town where Al's father set out on a variety of moneymaking ventures—growing vegetables and selling timber, groceries, and real estate.

Samuel Edison had one idea that set the family apart in the community. He built a 100-foot-tall (30 m) wooden stairway structure in their yard. For 25 cents, people could climb the stairs to the top, where they could see the view for miles. Neighbors made fun of the "Edison Tower," but Samuel claimed it was a joke that paid. Al learned firsthand how to create something of value that people would pay to use. Years later he said people would pay well for entertainment, something he first realized as he helped his father collect coins from the townspeople.

Al and his parents worked hard in Port Huron. Al worked on the family's 10-acre farm garden, growing corn, radishes, onions, parsnips, and beets. He and another boy did the work and then took a horse and wagon loaded with vegetables to town and sold them door-to-door. One year Al gave his mother $600—the equivalent of over $12,000 today—that he earned from the farm garden.

The Edison family home had six bedrooms, and Al's mother rented some of the spare rooms to boarders. Al learned the value of money and hard work while he was young, and that knowledge never left him. There was plenty of work to do, but Al's parents knew he needed to attend school, too. Nancy Edison had been among the first generation of young

MAKE A STEAM-POWERED BOAT

BEFORE STEAM-POWERED engines were invented, machinery was powered by moving water, such as rivers and streams. The water moved waterwheels, which powered equipment like sawmills, flour mills, and weaving looms. The moving water worked great—except when unpredictable weather caused the water to flow either too fast or too slow. And waterpower meant that all factories had to be built right next to waterways.

After Robert Fulton demonstrated his steam-powered boat in 1807, American industry took off in new directions. Steam power meant machinery could be located wherever there was something to burn, like wood or coal, to fuel the engine. Steamboats and steam locomotives could carry their fuel right along with them. Suddenly, American factories began spreading across the country. Steam power also meant that boats could easily move up rivers for the first time in history, and locomotives could deliver passengers and loads far from waterways.

⚡ **Adult supervision required**

YOU'LL NEED
※ Utility knife
※ Soft plastic bottle (such as the kind used for contact lens solution)
※ Small votive candle (the kind that sits in an aluminum cup)
※ Duct tape
※ ⅛-inch (.31-cm) diameter soft copper tubing
※ Tubing cutter or hacksaw
※ Knife or sandpaper
※ Large pen or pencil
※ Nail
※ Body of water (such as a pond or swimming pool)
※ Matches or lighter

Using the utility knife, cut the plastic bottle in half lengthwise. Place the candle near the bow (front) of the boat and secure it in place with a small amount of duct tape. Cut a 12-inch (30.4-cm) length of copper tubing with the tubing cutter or saw, and clean the debris out of the cut with a knife or sandpaper. Gently bend the tubing around a large pen or pencil to form a coil in the center, then remove the pen or pencil. Poke two holes in the stern (back) of the boat with a nail, and force the two ends of the copper tubes through the holes, forming a watertight fit. Carefully bend the tubing so the coil is just above the top of where the candle's flame will be.

Now you're ready to launch your steamboat. Place the boat in a body of water, and fill the copper tube with water by holding one end of the tube underwater and sucking gently on the other end. When the tube is full of water, make sure the boat is resting in the water with both ends of the tubing under the water, and light the candle. When the coil of copper tubing gets hot enough to boil the water inside, the boat will start moving forward. Put your fingers in the water just behind the tubes, and you can feel little pulses of water. These pulses are pushing the boat along.

How does this work? When the water in the coil boils, the steam expands and pushes the water out of the tube ends, propelling the boat forward. As the steam continues to expand, it encounters the section of tubing that was once full of water. This tubing is cold, and the steam condenses back into water. This causes a vacuum to form, which pulls more water back into the two ends of the tube. These two streams of water meet each other in the coil, pushing the boat forward and reversing any backward motion caused by the water being sucked into the tubes. This pulsing, back-and-forth water motion is rapid enough that the comparatively heavy boat never actually moves backward at all, only forward.

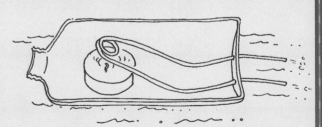

girls allowed to attend school long enough to become a teacher. But most school boards in those days had regulations stating that once a woman married, she could no longer work as a teacher. Nancy Edison had taught Al to read, write, and sketch. Now, she felt, her youngest child should go to school.

Unfortunately, before Al could enroll, he caught scarlet fever, an infectious disease common in the 1800s. Scarlet fever is caused by streptococcus bacteria and can be passed by an infected person's cough or by drinking milk from an infected cow. Scarlet fever causes a high body temperature, sickness, sore throat, and a scarlet rash that spreads over the body, even the tongue. A serious case can cause ear and kidney infections and swollen neck glands. Today, scarlet fever is cured with antibiotics; in the 1850s doctors gave herbal tonics and teas and mercury pills. No one knows how Al caught the disease or how sick he was, but it kept him from attending school until he was eight and a half years old.

Finally Al's parents enrolled him in Reverend George Engle's school, where he attended class with 15 other students. He also took piano lessons from Reverend Engle. The school was expensive, though, so his parents soon switched him to a public school, a crowded one-room school with 40 students between the ages of 5 and 21. But Al was not suited for school—he had difficulty learning his lessons and became easily distracted from his work. Schoolwork in those days meant memorizing facts or poems, then reciting them aloud without mistakes. There was never a chance to do or make anything. Al said he needed to see things with his own eyes, to make and do things and try them out for himself. He said that trying something out for himself was "better than learning about something he had never seen."

Teachers were very strict and often swatted students who made mistakes or misbehaved. The teacher frequently slapped and ridiculed Al in front of the class. One day Al heard the schoolmaster, Mr. Crawford, say that Al was "addled" and that it was useless to keep him in school. Addled was a term used for students who had problems learning. Al's feelings were hurt. He rushed home crying and begged his mother not to make him go back to school.

Mrs. Edison was furious. Edison recalled, "I found out what a good thing a mother was; she brought me back to the school and angrily told the teacher that he didn't know what he was talking about. She was the most enthusiastic champion a boy ever had, and I determined right then that I would be worthy of her, and show her that her confidence had not been misplaced."

This drawing of Reverend Engle's school was made by a classmate.

Al's formal schooling had lasted only three months. From that point on, he was home-schooled by his mother. She finished her housework in the morning, then sat down with Al and went over lessons with him. She had him read books meant for adults, such as books of world history and works by Shakespeare and Dickens. By the age of nine, Al was reading such adult books by himself.

In reality, though, Al's mother wasn't teaching him anything—he was teaching himself. She found books on subjects he was interested in, such as science, and didn't make him work too hard on things he didn't like, such as spelling and arithmetic. "My mother was the making of me," he said. "She understood me; she let me follow my bent [interests]."

There were few laws requiring children to attend school at that time. The first compulsory attendance law was adopted in Massachusetts in 1852. After the Civil War, other states followed suit, but it wasn't until 1918 that all states required children to attend school. Most children didn't get the chance because they were working. They worked on farms or in mines or factories. Most children went to school for only a few months of the year in the winter, and few went beyond the sixth grade. There were few high schools or academies to prepare students for colleges, and a lack of schooling seldom held anyone

back in life. Learning basic reading, writing, and math skills was enough for most people. Al quickly learned the basics at home and began reading his parents' books. His parents encouraged him to read—in fact, for a while his father paid the boy for every book he read. He enjoyed reading throughout his life, and later when he was a successful inventor he would order hundreds of dollars of books at a time—telling a New York City bookstore to send him every book on a particular subject he wanted to learn about.

One book in particular shaped Edison's life. It was called *A School Compendium of Natural and Experimental Philosophy*, or *Parker's Philosophy*. It described electricity, batteries, magnetism, how steam engines worked, and how the telegraph worked. The book was filled with details on simple experiments. Using the book to guide him, Al set out making many machines: some to create electricity, others friction, others magnetic action. The book and the experiments he did from it laid the research foundation he followed for the rest of his life.

Parker's Philosophy also had a chart of the Morse Telegraphic Alphabet, or "Morse code," which telegraphers used to send messages over telegraph lines with electric impulses. It used

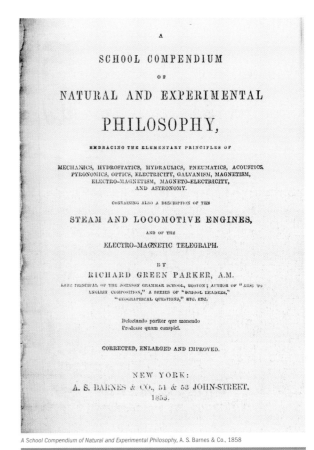

A School Compendium of Natural and Experimental Philosophy, A. S. Barnes & Co., 1858

This is the cover of a textbook Al read as a boy. *Parker's Philosophy* **was a popular schoolbook for decades.**

ELECTRIC AMBER

THE WORD FOR "electricity" comes from the word "electron," the Greek word for amber. Amber is a smooth piece of fossilized tree resin. Ancient Greeks found that rubbing a piece of amber made it attract light materials like feathers, which moved through the air to cling to it. It seemed magical, and no one could explain it. Those early amber experiments were the foundation of electrical research.

dots and dashes to represent letters of the alphabet, making it possible to send messages in code, to be decoded by a telegrapher and written down on paper in English.

Al taught himself the Morse code and wanted to be a telegrapher, a new job using a new technology that was sweeping the country. Like computer programming today, telegraphy used its own language and was like no other type of study. It was fresh, exciting, and full of opportunities. It also meant that people had to learn to think about communicating in entirely different ways. Dots and dashes—sent by electric pulses over a wire—represented words. People no longer had to wait days or weeks for a letter to arrive; they could send a telegram and receive a reply immediately. All it took was a telegrapher on the receiving end to interpret the coded clicks of the telegraph key.

Another subject that fascinated young Al Edison was chemistry, and he continued to read chemistry books most of his life. He loved to mix chemicals together to study their reactions. He used the information from books to perform many experiments on his own. He gathered up things such as feathers, sulfur, beeswax, cornstalk pitch, acids, alum, and just about anything else he could find that could

be useful in an experiment. He collected glass jars and ceramic dishes, bits of wood and metal, springs, and wires. With a good collection to tinker with, he worked out inventions and projects from his books and came up with ideas of his own.

He enjoyed reading, but he liked making things even more. He said that most kids "were interested in knowing how things are done." He worked on chemistry and telegraphy experiments and built a variety of other projects. He made water mills, a cannon, and a little steam engine railroad that he set up in one room of the house. Al gathered over 200 empty bottles and jars and filled them with chemicals and materials he collected. He bought his chemicals and equipment with money he earned selling vegetables and newspapers.

Mrs. Edison sometimes got upset about the mess. The dangerous chemicals left stains and odors, and the wet-cell batteries leaked sulphuric acid, which ate holes in the furniture and the floor. "My mother's ideas and mine differed at times, especially when I got experimenting and mussed up things," he said. When he was 10 years old, his mother made him move everything to the basement. Al labeled every bottle "Poison" so no one would touch his collection, and eventually his mother made him keep the basement door locked when he wasn't working there.

MAKE AN ELECTRICALLY CHARGED PUPPET DANCE

SIMILAR TO one of the activities in *Parker's Philosophy,* this project shows how electrical charges can cause an object to move. You can make this puppet easily from white plastic grocery bags—it almost looks like a ghost dancing in the air.

YOU'LL NEED
* 3 thin plastic bags, like the kind found in the vegetable department of the grocery store
* 12-inch (30.4-cm) dowel
* Rubber band
* Scissors
* Balloon

A School Compendium of Natural and Experimental Philosophy, A. S. Barnes & Co., 1858

Here's how the dancing puppet project appeared in Parker's book. The strips were cut from tissue paper.

Roll up one bag to make a ball for the puppet's head. Slip the other two bags over the ball, and fasten them to the end of the dowel with a rubber band wrapped several times tightly around the dowel. Use scissors to cut the bags into thin strips, about one-half-inch wide. Blow up the balloon and tie the end closed. Rub the balloon over your hair several times to charge it with electric ions. Then hold the puppet near the balloon, and watch it "dance." The electrons are attracting the pieces of plastic bag, pulling them like a magnet.

You just created static electricity that builds up on objects. It's not the same electricity that moves through wires—that's current electricity. Here's how static electricity works: everything is made up of very tiny particles called atoms. Atoms have even smaller particles, called protons, neutrons, and electrons. Protons have a positive charge, electrons have a negative charge, and neutrons have no charge at all. They are usually in equal numbers, so they are balanced.

The basic rule of electricity is that like charges repel, unlike charges attract. When you first touched the balloon (with its negative charges) near your hair (with its negative charges), the hair moved away from the balloon slightly (like charges repel). After rubbing the balloon onto your hair, the hair's protons became positively charged. With its

new positive charge, the hair was attracted to the balloon's atoms because they were now opposites (the balloon remained negatively charged). Rub the balloon on your hair a bit longer, and the protons move from the hair onto the balloon, and the balloon becomes positively charged. When you moved the positively charged balloon to the plastic, the negatively charged electrons in the plastic were attracted to the positive protons in the balloon (unlike charges attract). But the balloon and plastic can't hold the charges for long. After a while the protons move from the balloon to the plastic, while negative electrons drop off and the materials lose their attraction for each other because they have the same charges.

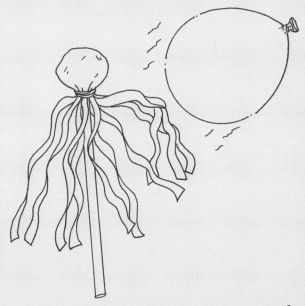

THE SEEDS OF INVENTION

THESE ILLUSTRATIONS are from some experiments shown in *Parker's Philosophy,* which Al read with interest. The one on the left shows how a Magic Lantern projector worked. The one on the right shows an invention for recording telegraph messages. When he was an adult, Edison created inventions that seem to have their roots in these drawings: the moving picture projector and the phonograph. These ideas may have been stuck in his mind since his childhood and been helpful in figuring out how to solve invention problems he worked on as an adult.

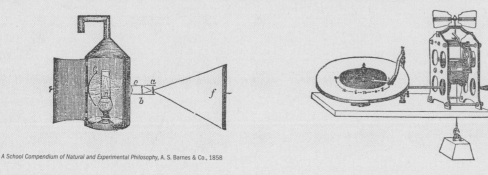

A School Compendium of Natural and Experimental Philosophy, A. S. Barnes & Co., 1858

His experiments often went awry and caused problems for others. Once, he and some friends tried some experiments in a telegraph office, created an explosion, and blew out part of the building. Another time, he talked his friend Michael Oates into drinking a potion made of Seidlitz powder, which he thought might make his friend able to fly. Seidlitz powder was a common laxative, made from baking soda, tartaric acid, and potassium sodium tartrate. Oates got very sick, and Mrs. Edison spanked her son soundly.

The family cats were favorite subjects for Al's experiments, too. He had read about Benjamin Franklin's discoveries about static electricity and tried to rub the fur of the two cats, whose tails he had attached to wires. He didn't get far with the experiment before he was clawed.

Al's father worried because the boy spent so much time alone in the basement. "He spent the greater part of his time in the cellar," he said. "He did not share to any extent the sports of his neighborhood. He never knew a real boyhood like other boys." He couldn't understand how Al could find his lonely experiments interesting. Al, however, was happy to be able to tinker on things in his laboratory. Once in a while there would be a muffled explosion and the parents would worry. "He will blow us all up!" his father would exclaim. "Let him be," his mother advised, "Al knows what he's about."

Not much is known about the Edison family's traditions or activities. Most likely, they were very much like other families in those days. There was one practice they followed, however, which may have set them apart. Because medicine was poorly developed, people tried to prevent illness any way they could. The Edisons followed a strict diet, hoping to remain healthy. Al's father had been raised on the diet by his parents and continued the family tradition based on a diet book written 300 years earlier by an Italian nobleman, Luigi Cornaro. Cornaro's diet was described in his book *The Art of Living Long* and was popular for several hundred years. What was his secret? He advised people to eat very little food.

Al's father and grandfather followed the diet, hoping to attain long life by eating little. "Morning, noon, and night I was told to leave the table while still hungry," Al said. "I do not remember whether, in the beginning, it was hard to do this, but, in any event, I soon became accustomed to it."

Until the 1920s and 1930s, little was known about the body and how it metabolized or even digested foods. Vitamins hadn't been discovered when Edison was young, and neither had protein or carbohydrates. People thought that eating a lot of something was good for you. But most people didn't become overweight because they didn't eat prepared foods. Everything was cooked from scratch—canned foods weren't available. Soda pop, made with sugar, hadn't been invented yet, either.

Al spent hours sketching out his ideas or drawing things he saw in his notebooks. He continued to sketch his ideas, cartoons, and doodles for the rest of his life, eventually filling hundreds of notebooks. But just because he spent so much time with his ideas, books, and experiments didn't mean Al stayed out of mischief. He was known in the family and neighborhood as a charming, happy boy, but also a bit of a troublemaker. His cousin, 13-year-old Nancy, babysat him and said while he was usually a good boy he could be very stubborn if he didn't get his own way.

Al and some friends formed a secret club and dug tunnels and a cave with a hidden trapdoor and built a dungeon that they filled with a table, chairs, and food. They called themselves the "north side boys" and their rivals, the "south side boys," met in another spot. Al and friends got into trouble for playing tricks on the volunteer troops stationed near his house at Fort Gratiot. The Civil War had begun, and the soldiers spent their time drilling and marching, calling out commands and orders. Al and his friends observed everything, then hid in the dark of night and called out confusing commands to the sentinels (the soldiers on watch). When the soldiers came looking for him, Al hid in a barrel of apples in the basement. The next morning, his father gave him a good switching on the legs. He decided it was time to put the lively boy to work.

EATING HABITS

WHEN THOMAS Alva Edison had children of his own, he tried to get them to follow the ideas presented in Luigi Cornaro's *The Art of Living Long*. His father lived to be 92 years old and Thomas Edison lived to be 84. The life expectancy for most men in Edison's time was around 50, so perhaps the diet worked! As a grown-up, Edison ate whatever foods he wanted, but only four to six ounces at a time (the equivalent of about a cup of soup or a thick slice of cheese and two slices of bread). He took pride in eating small amounts at meals and believed that Americans could cut down their food intake by two-thirds. "They do the work of a 3-horse-power engine and consume the fuel which should operate 50-horse-power engines." In 1930, a year before he died, Edison adopted an even more unusual diet in which he limited his meals to seven glasses of milk and one orange each day. Perhaps the diet weakened his health. What was Edison's favorite food for most of his life? Apple dumplings or apple pie, with a glass of milk.

The Mt. Clemens, Michigan, train station where young Edison sold newspapers
and learned the skill of telegraphy played a major part in shaping his life.

MOUNT CLEMENS

Time to Get Moving

2

> "THE HAPPIEST TIME OF MY
> LIFE WAS WHEN I WAS 12 YEARS OLD.
> I WAS JUST OLD ENOUGH TO HAVE
> A GOOD TIME IN THE WORLD, BUT
> NOT OLD ENOUGH TO UNDERSTAND
> ANY OF ITS TROUBLES."
> —THOMAS EDISON

Al Hits the Rails

WHILE YOUNG Al Edison was busy working out his experiments, the nation was undergoing a major shift from using water and animals for transportation to using railways. Railways moved faster, and rail lines could be laid just about anywhere. Canal lines were soon forgotten. A Canadian rail line built a depot at Port Huron, connecting the town to the growing link of rail lines spreading over North America. Along with railroads came telegraph lines, which linked people and places with a new communications technology.

In 1859, the Grand Trunk Railroad extended its line north to Port Huron from Detroit. The new railroad depot was down the hill from the Edison home, and the bustle and excitement of trains, passengers, and freight lured 12-year-old Al. Like many boys at the time, he decided he wanted to be a railroad engineer when he grew up.

The stationmaster offered him a job painting signs around the station, because he could sketch and draw so well. But Al decided to work as a "candy butcher" instead, selling newspapers, magazines, and snacks to the passengers. He didn't receive a wage but made whatever profit he could by selling these items, which he purchased himself. Al's father was glad of the opportunity for the boy to make some money. Edison later recalled, "Being poor, I already knew that money is a valuable thing." Al convinced his reluctant mother to let him take the job when he told her how much reading he could get done while waiting over in Detroit every day. And besides, he said, the money he could earn would fund his experiments.

Every morning at 7:00 A.M. the train pulled out of Port Huron with Al aboard. He sold the passengers newspapers, books, sandwiches, figs, apples, candy, peanuts, cigars—whatever might keep them from boredom or hunger during the three-hour ride to Detroit.

Once the train reached Detroit, Al was free to find something to do until the return trip in the evening. He spent hours at the Detroit Public Library and was one of its earliest members, paying two dollars (an amount equal to a week's wages in those days) for library card number 33. "My refuge was the Detroit Public Library," he said. "I started with the first book on the bottom shelf and went through the lot, one by one. I didn't read a few books. I read the library."

He also wandered the streets of Detroit, which had a population of about 25,000 then, watching workers in machine shops, telegraph offices, and the train yard. But he soon tired of wandering around and got permission to build a small laboratory for experiments in the baggage car of the train. While the train sat in Detroit all day, Al could busy himself with his favorite activity, chemistry. He quickly filled shelves with bottles, test tubes, and batteries.

The days were long, and the train moved slowly—only 30 miles (48 km) an hour—not returning to Port Huron until 9:00 P.M. During the ride Al sometimes sat in the engine car and got to work some of the controls or shovel coal into the firebox to keep the engine hot. When he was 13, an engineer let him drive a freight train for over 60 miles (97 km)—something many people yearned to do!

Al was a busy entrepreneur. He set up two sales stands in Port Huron. One sold magazines and newspapers, and the other sold butter, berries, and vegetables. He hired two boys to work at them, paying them with a share of the profits. One boy cheated him out of some money, so he closed that newspaper stand, but he ran the vegetable stand for a year, buying vegetables to sell when he ran out of garden items. He also bought butter and blackberries from farmers along the rail line and sold them to railroad employees' wives. When the railroad opened up another route, he hired a boy to sell newspapers and candy on it. He was a busy salesman and employer—while still young himself.

He usually earned 8 or 10 dollars a day—a huge amount at that time, equivalent to over $160 today. He gave his mother a dollar a day, and spent the rest on chemicals, batteries, books, and laboratory supplies.

The Telegraph Beckons

Telegraphy was a mysterious new technology, and every train station had a telegraph office to pass messages about incoming trains as well as spread news. Everyone was excited about sending instant messages and Al, too, wanted to be part of the new communication

TEST SOLUTIONS IN YOUR OWN CHEMISTRY LAB

ONE USEFUL test that chemists and others do is testing a solution to see how much acid it holds. Testing for acidity is important for keeping swimming pools clean, for checking levels of sugar in the body of a person with diabetes, and for gardeners who want to test soils to create the best growing conditions for plants. Chemists use a special paper, called litmus paper, which changes color when dipped in a solution. A chemical reaction between the paper and the solution causes it to darken to orange or red if the solution has a high level of acidity. Or, if the solution is not acidic, but alkaline, the paper turns shades of green or blue. Acidity or alkalinity levels are measured as pH (meaning the power of hydrogen).

Al Edison did many experiments like this one, testing liquids to see whether they were acidic or not. He always recorded his findings in case the results might be useful for some future project.

YOU'LL NEED
* Package of litmus paper (available in drug stores or from Edmund Scientific—see Supply Sources at back of this book)
* Water
* Several glasses
* Spoon
* Materials to test: vinegar, milk, sugar, salt, soda pop, orange juice, baking soda, lemon juice (about 1 tablespoon of each)
* Paper and pencil to record results

Treat the litmus paper strips carefully: don't expose them to air or moisture or they won't be accurate. Keep them inside their package, removing each strip as you begin to test with it.

Pour water into a glass until the glass is about half full. Add a spoonful of vinegar to the water and stir to mix. Dip one end of a test paper into the solution and pull it out quickly—don't let it soak. Watch it change color. The litmus paper package will have a color chart, showing the different levels of acidity and alkalinity. Match your paper's color to the chart. Now record your results on paper. Repeat the process to test other materials.

era. There weren't schools that taught telegraphy, but Al and a friend, Jimmy Clancy, built a telegraph using the ideas in the Parker book. The line was about a half mile long between their homes, made of common stovepipe wire strung on trees and short poles. The boys used bottles hung on nails as insulators to keep the wire from touching the poles. They needed a source of electricity to send the messages over the wire, so they bought batteries. They taught themselves Morse code (using the Parker book) and tried to send messages back and forth. It worked!

Since Al was away at work all day, the only time the boys could practice with their telegraph was at night. But Al's father refused to allow him to stay up late after returning from selling newspapers all day on the train. The boys found a way around that, though. Samuel Edison eagerly looked forward to getting leftover newspapers each evening so he could catch up on the news. When there weren't any leftover papers, Al told his father they could use the homemade telegraph to find out what the news was. The Clancys subscribed to a newspaper, and using Morse code and their simple contraption, the boys relayed news headlines over the telegraph wire, impressing Mr. Edison so much he let Al stay up until midnight most evenings to send and receive messages after work. This lasted until a stray cow wandering through the orchard got caught up in the wires and tore them down.

At about this time, when Al was between 12 and 13 years old, he began to notice problems with his hearing. It was probably a result of the many ear infections he'd had as a child, as well as the scarlet fever. Because antibiotics were not available, it was possible that those infections could have damaged his ability to hear. He couldn't hear birds sing and couldn't hear people talking quietly. Working on the train was fine, though, because the noise was loud and everyone shouted. He realized he would never be able to attend school again because he couldn't hear the teacher. Life was difficult for a person with a disability in those years, and there was no way for Al to improve his hearing. He felt shut off from small talk and friends, and turned to reading for hours at the library to amuse himself. "Deafness probably drove me to reading," he explained.

In 1862 the Civil War was raging. Michigan was far from the battle lines, but local men had gone to fight in the Union army and everyone wanted to know what was happening on the battlefront. This was before radio and television, so newspapers were the only way to find out what was happening in the rest of the nation. Al sold as many as he could, but he had to be careful not to purchase more newspapers than he could sell, or he lost money that day. He watched his customers carefully, to see what sort of news sold best. Events connected to the war were in the news every day, but he soon noticed that newspapers sold better when they carried news of battles. He started going to the newspaper workroom, where the typesetters were laying out the headlines with pieces of lead type, to learn what headlines they were putting on that day's edition of the newspaper. That way he could decide how many newspapers to buy to take on the train. He was becoming a shrewd businessman.

On April 6, 1862, Al arrived on the train in Detroit to hear the news that a huge battle (the Battle of Shiloh) had taken place, with thousands dead or wounded, but no one had any idea who had won. The telegraph operators who learned about it first said there had been 60,000 killed. Al knew the headlines would be exciting and everyone would want to learn the details. He quickly realized it was a great opportunity to sell more newspapers than usual. He said he knew people would be "eager for the newspapers telling how sixty thousand men had fallen among the armies of the North and South." He decided to work up

interest in buying newspapers by sending word back down the rail line to each station about the big news. "Here was a chance for enormous sales, if only the people along the line could know what had happened," he realized. He offered to give a telegraph operator free magazines for three months in exchange

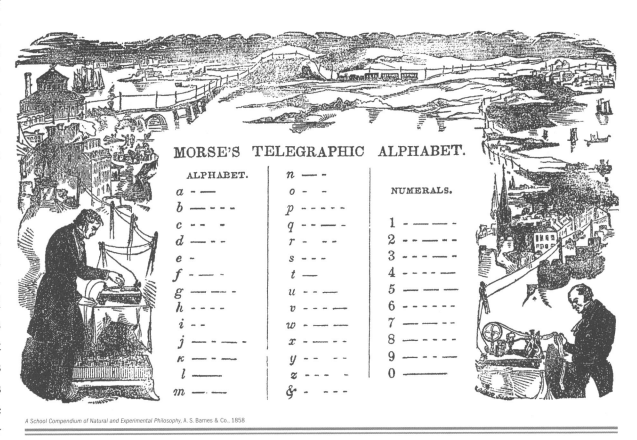

A School Compendium of Natural and Experimental Philosophy, A. S. Barnes & Co., 1858

This is the Morse Telegraphic Alphabet used by telegraphers to send messages by clicking to match the code.

for sending a message over the telegraph to the stations along the line back to Port Huron. He asked each stationmaster to post a sign telling about the battle and that newspapers would soon arrive with the details.

Then he had to figure out how to get more newspapers than usual. He thought he could sell a thousand papers that day, but he had no money to pay for them. He met with the editor of the *Detroit Free Press* and paid for 300 copies. After some convincing, the editor gave him the rest on credit. "I was a pretty cheeky boy, and I felt desperate," he admitted. He hired another boy to help him, and they lugged the newspapers back to the train, where they had to fold each one. Al set out on the return trip that day with high hopes—and lots of newspapers he now had to sell. Would his plan work? It was a risk, but one he figured would be successful.

At the first station, Utica, where he usually sold two newspapers, a crowd waited on the platform. He sold 35 papers. "I realized that the telegraph was a great invention," he said. If demand like that continued, he knew he wouldn't have enough papers, so he decided to raise the price at the next station. At every stop, a crowd was waiting and eagerly paid twice the usual price for his newspapers. By the time he reached Port Huron, he was getting 25 cents for each newspaper, which usu-ally sold for a nickel, calling out to the crowd, "Twenty-five cents, gentlemen—I haven't enough to go around!" The excitement interrupted a prayer meeting next door, and the church members rallied around, bidding against one another for the newspapers.

"It was then it struck me that the telegraph was just about the best thing going, for it was the notices on the bulletin board that had done the trick," he said. "I determined at once to become a telegrapher."

Because he was always trying to figure out the proper number of newspapers to purchase for resale, and often miscalculated (except for the Battle of Shiloh success), it wasn't long before Al decided he could make more profit by selling his own newspaper. He rearranged his laboratory in the rail car and created a newspaper printing office of his own. He bought an old printing press in Detroit, 300 pounds (136 kg) of lead type, and paper, and learned how to compose and set type, run a printing press, and publish his own newspaper. He wrote and printed a weekly newspaper, which he called the *Weekly Herald,* to sell on the train. He reported the news and events going on along the rail route between Detroit and Port Huron. The paper included news stories from Detroit as well as gossip and some corny jokes. He sold it for three cents a copy—or eight cents a month for a subscription. In no time he was printing and selling 400 copies per issue. It was a genuine newspaper. Al got news stories from the telegraph offices so it had the most up-to-date information and included stories about the railway workers and their activities as well. The railroad company highly approved, and Al's newspaper was written about in a major London newspaper, which reported it was the only newspaper ever printed on a moving train. As a newspaper writer and printer, Al earned another 20 to 30 dollars each month.

Al's railcar laboratory–printing office ended up creating problems for him. One day the train hit a bad piece of track and the cars lurched forward. The motion threw some phosphorus onto the floor of the baggage car, where it burst into flame and ignited the wooden floor. Al was throwing water on the flames when the train conductor came in, saw his burning baggage car, and jumped in to quench the flames. The conductor was furious and threw Al, his laboratory, and the printing press off the train at the next stop.

Unhappy but not defeated, Al dragged his belongings home, where he set up again in the family basement. He continued printing the *Weekly Herald* from home and even started another paper that was full of gossip (like today's

tabloids) called *Paul Pry*. There are no copies of that paper in existence, but whatever Al printed, it angered one fellow so much that the outraged man threw Al into the river. Al soon quit publishing his own newspapers and went back to selling other editors' newspapers.

One more adventure filled the year 1862, when Al rescued a child from a train. He'd been standing on the platform at the Mt. Clemens, Michigan, station selling papers while train cars were shuffled up and down the tracks to connect for the remainder of the trip. One loose boxcar came rolling toward a three-year-old child playing on the tracks. Al dashed out, grabbed the boy, and saved him from the car. The child's father, J. U. Mackenzie, was the stationmaster, and to show his gratitude to Al, he offered to teach him telegraphy.

Al jumped at the chance. He hired another boy to take over half of his newspaper route and moved in with the Mackenzie family as a boarder so he could take telegraphy lessons from Mr. Mackenzie at night. During the daytime he continued with part of the newspaper route and hung around the station, helping Mr. Mackenzie with his duties. Al was 15 years old, and knew this was his chance of a lifetime to learn the important new skill of telegraphy.

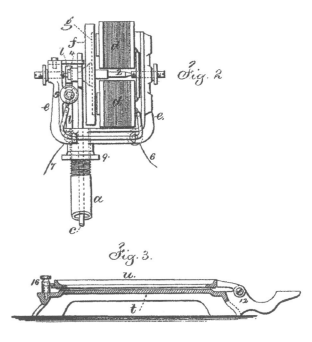

It was a lucky break. Because telegraphy was so new, it wasn't taught in schools. Learning it required working as an apprentice with someone who knew how to do it. During the Civil War, telegraphy swept the country as railroads in the North feverishly laid down more tracks. Telegraph wires were strung along railroad lines, and messages were sent over the wires between towns, cities, and rail stations. There was a great need for skilled operators, and many young men and women (telegraphy was one of the first technical professions open to women) were eager to learn telegraphy and to work in the new field.

Al already knew Morse code, which was the telegraphic alphabet, but telegraphers also used special signals for numbers and abbreviations, which Al needed to learn. For example, "73" meant "good wishes," and "23" meant an accident or death message. It took Al only three or four months to master the system, and as with everything he did, he worked extremely hard at it. He made up his own set of telegraph instruments at a gunsmith's shop, using bits of spring, brass, and metal he collected from trash.

Operating a telegraph seems like it would be difficult for someone like Al, who had lost much of his ability to hear. He said it was easy, though. "I had found that my deafness did not prevent me from hearing the clicking of a telegraph instrument," he said. "From the start I found that deafness was an advantage to a telegrapher. While I could hear unerr-

Dover Publications

The scene at the Battle of Shiloh during the Civil War.

ingly the loud ticking of the instrument, I could not hear other and perhaps distracting sounds."

Having learned to "take copy"—write down on paper the words that the clicked code symbolized—Al looked for an opportunity to make money from his new skill. The Port Huron telegraph operator left his job to join the U.S. Military Telegraph Corps, and Al was hired to take his place, as an apprentice. The telegraph office was in the back of a jeweler's shop, and Al set up a cot in the back of the room and went to work. The job didn't last long. The jeweler didn't like Al tinkering with his fine tools, and Al's father wouldn't let him sign apprentice papers for less than $25 a month; the job paid only $20.

Al stayed at the telegraph office nearly day and night, taking down the news messages that came over the wires until 3:00 A.M. During the night fewer messages came over the wire so he was able to practice and improve his speed. The telegraph fascinated him, and he questioned other operators about how it worked—but none were sure. One fellow told him it was like having a very long dachshund dog—if you pulled on its tail in one town, it barked in another. How the electrical pulses went through the wire remained a mystery to most people.

One winter an ice jam built up in Lake Erie. The huge blocks of floating ice tore apart the underwater telegraph cable running between Port Huron and the Canadian shore across the lake, and all telegrams between the two ceased. Al did some creative thinking and enlisted a railroad engineer to blast the locomotive whistle in Morse code, which was picked up by a listening telegrapher on the Canadian side. That earned Al some local fame as a telegrapher, which helped him get a better job as a railroad telegrapher at a nearby station for the Grand Trunk Railroad, across the border in Canada. He liked the job because he could work nights and experiment with his chemicals in his boardinghouse room in the daytime.

As a night telegrapher, Al caught up on his sleep by napping when no telegrams came over the wire during the night. Night operators were required to send a signal to the office of the train dispatcher at certain times during the night, to show they were on duty (and not sleeping!). Al devised a clever invention that worked like a clock. It was based on a wheel with notched edges that at certain hours sent the required message to the train office. It worked just fine until the train manager tried to contact Al a few times during the night and got no answer. A visit by the

MAKE AN ELECTRIC TELEGRAPH MACHINE

THE TELEGRAPH works by sending electric current over a wire. The message is sent by breaking the current into short (dot) and long (dash) bursts. You and a partner can communicate with the Morse code using your own machine.

YOU'LL NEED

* 2 brass paper fasteners
* 2-by-2-inch (5-by-5-cm) piece of cardboard
* Paper clip
* Scissors
* 3 12-inch (30.4-cm) pieces of insulated wire (sometimes sold as bell wire)
* 3-volt buzzer (sold in hobby and craft stores and electronics stores)
* 6-volt alkaline lantern battery (sold in hardware and grocery stores)

TO MAKE THE SWITCH

Push the fasteners into the cardboard so their prongs protrude through the other side, about 1½ inches (3.8 cm) apart. Bend the end of the paper clip and slip it around one of the fasteners so it bends slightly upward. With scissors, gently remove the insulation from about 1 inch (2.5 cm) at the ends of all three 12-inch (30.4-cm) wire pieces. It works best to gently cut into the plastic covering and then pull it away with your fingernails.

Be careful not to cut through the wires. Twist one end of one 12-inch (30.4-cm) wire tightly around one fastener head, and one end of the second 12-inch (30.4-cm) wire around the other fastener head. (The third 12-inch wire will be used later.) Press the fastener heads firmly against the cardboard and spread their prongs apart on the other side of the cardboard. This will be the switch.

TO ATTACH THE BUZZER

Strip away about a half-inch of plastic insulation from the ends of the two wires that are attached to the buzzer. Wrap the end of one buzzer wire around the end of one of the 12-inch (30.4-cm) wires that connects to a brass fastener (the one without the paper clip) on the switch you made. Wrap the end of the wire that connects to the other brass fastener (the one with the paper clip) around

one of the two battery posts on the battery. Take the last 12-inch-long (30.4-cm) piece of wire and wrap one end around the second battery post and the other end around the end of the remaining buzzer wire. Screw the battery caps down to hold the wires in place around the battery posts.

To complete the circuit, press down on the paper clip so it touches the opposite brass fastener. The buzzer will sound every time you connect the circuit. The electric current that is stored in the battery runs from the battery posts, along the wires. When the current is interrupted, or broken, it can't travel. When the metal paper clip touches the metal fastener, the current can pass through the metals, creating a circuit that rings the buzzer. To send messages in code, use the Morse code below to tap out short (dot) and long (dash) signals on the buzzer.

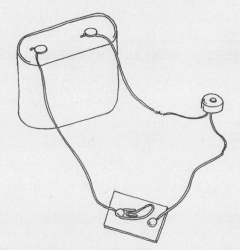

THE MORSE CODE				
A ·—	G ——·	M ——	S ···	Y —·——
B —···	H ····	N —·	T —	Z ——··
C —·—·	I ··	O ———	U ··—	
D —··	J ·———	P ·——·	V ···—	
E ·	K —·—	Q ——·—	W ·——	
F ··—·	L ·—··	R ·—·	X —··—	

manager revealed his shortcut and he was reprimanded.

Al threw out the homemade signal device and instead asked a night watchman to wake him before the set times, so he could go to the telegraph table and send the necessary signals during the night. One night he nearly missed a message telling him to stop a train at the station because another train was on its way on the same tracks from the opposite direction. When he alerted the signalman, he learned the fellow had already given the engineer the go-ahead. Al raced after the train, trying to stop it before the two engines collided head-on. Fortunately, the engineers saw each other on a straight stretch of track and were able to stop their trains in time.

The train manager suspected Al had been neglecting his duty and caused the near-collision, and the next day Al was called into the manager's office. Neglect of duty was a criminal offense for railroad employees because it could result in disastrous wrecks and potential deaths. In Canada, it could mean a prison sentence. As Al was meeting with the angry manager, a group of important business visitors arrived and distracted the manager. In the commotion, Al snuck out and hopped a ride on a freight train, making his way home to Michigan.

Union Army telegraph operators sitting in camp. Telegraph lines were strung between the general's tent on the battlefield and the local train station, linking the army to a network that made communication fast and easy during the Civil War.

Library of Congress, LC B8171-7358

3

Wandering and Working

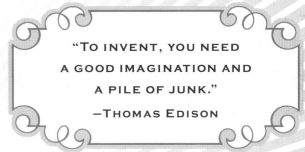

On the Way to Invention

DURING 1864, 17-year-old Al Edison held four different telegraphy jobs in four different towns. He moved from Michigan to Indiana to Ohio, getting fired for not doing his duties or not paying attention, or quitting as the months flew by. He would cut into the line to send messages, interrupting other messages when he felt his was more important, or let outgoing messages pile up while he read a book. He was always trying to devise inventions to make his job less work, or making gadgets to play practical jokes on other people.

For the next five years, Al roamed the Midwest, working at one telegraph job after another. He was young, footloose, and looking for opportunities and adventure. The Union army hired 1,500 telegraphers during the Civil War, and the Confederate army hired hundreds as well. After the war ended, railroad construction kept up a steady demand for telegraph operators at every rail station.

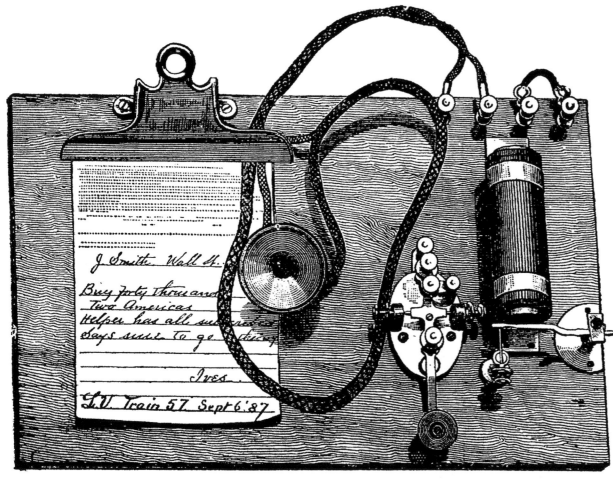

Dover Publications

Telegraphers' equipment for taking and sending messages in the Morse Alphabet.

Young men who took up telegraphy and moved about became known as "tramp operators." They quit jobs frequently because it was easy to find another, they were paid very well, and they often partied away their money, moving on to new jobs whenever they felt like it. As a tramp operator, young Edison enjoyed the freedom to travel, and he also made many friends he kept for years. The good pay appealed to him as he used it to purchase supplies for experiments, which he kept in his boardinghouse room.

Around this time Edison began going by his first name, Tom. Because he was living in boardinghouses with other young men like himself, he wasn't as well groomed as he should have been. He was thin from the haphazard diet and night work, and his hair was uncombed. His clothes hung too big on his frame and he wore a soiled paper collar, rather than a clean shirt. (Paper collars and cuffs were cheap ways for men to appear well-dressed, without bothering to pay a laundress to wash and iron a white shirt.)

Living in boardinghouses meant it was hard to keep a consistent working laboratory, but Tom always carted a pile of supplies and materials with him, setting them up in his room. Tools, rolls of wire, batteries, bottles of chemicals, books, scrap metal—he scrounged for things and used his earnings to buy what he couldn't find or make. After buying expensive laboratory equipment, he often didn't have enough money left to pay for his meals and would borrow money from friends.

Tom was improving his skills as a telegrapher, able to transmit long messages at a speed of 45 words a minute. As Tom became better at taking down messages, he pushed himself to write quickly. He taught himself to read faster, too, training himself to see print as several words at once. He always believed that speed reading should be taught in schools because it allowed him to easily read two or three books a day.

Telegraphers had to recognize and write down as many as 40 words a minute when messages were coming quickly. Sometimes it was too hard to keep up, so Tom invented a device to help him. He made a disk of paper that turned so marks could be pushed into it as it moved. As the dots and dashes came over the wire, they made marks on the paper. Tom could later go over the marks on the disk at a slower speed, so he didn't miss words that came too quickly for him to write down. He and another telegrapher used the device to turn out perfect copy until a supervisor discovered what they were doing and made them stop. Years later, Edison used the ideas behind that little device to create the phonograph.

Because telegraph offices were in warehouse districts and railroad stations, the neighborhoods and buildings were often run-down. The operators had to battle vermin like rats, mice, cockroaches, and lice. Always one to think up a clever solution to a problem, Tom made a "cockroach killer" by pasting two strips of tinfoil to the wall above his desk and connecting wires to the foil pieces leading to the positive and negative poles on one of the large batteries that powered the telegraph wires. Cockroaches walked on the strips, and when their legs were on both strips at the same time, the electricity surged through the roaches and fried them in a flash of light and puff of smoke. Tom's cockroach killer was such a hit the local newspaper printed a story about it. So many visitors came to watch it in action that his irritated boss made him stop using it.

Tom always looked for ways to make money. He enjoyed attending plays (there were no movies yet) and realized there was money to be made by copying the scripts. Because there were no copy machines (or typewriters), anything that had to be duplicated had to be handwritten. Making copies of a play for every member of the cast meant hours of tedious hand copying. The work appealed to

SWITCH ON AN ELECTRIC CURRENT TO MOVE A MAGNETIC FIELD

YOU CAN DO this experiment to watch how current flows through wires, then watch its effect on a compass needle. Magnets are attracted to the earth's magnetic North Pole, and a compass needle always moves to point north. An electric current can make the magnet move, however, because magnetism and electricity are closely connected. Try this simple experiment to see how electricity can affect magnetism.

YOU'LL NEED
* 2 brass paper fasteners
* 2-by-2-inch (5-by-5-cm) piece of cardboard
* Paper clip
* Scissors
* 2 1-foot- (30.5-cm) long pieces of wire
* 9-volt alkaline battery
* Battery clip (available in hardware or electronics stores)
* Compass

TO MAKE THE SWITCH
Push the fasteners into the cardboard, about 1½ inches (3.8 cm) apart. Bend the end of the paper clip and slip it around one of the fasteners so it bends slightly upward. With scissors, gently remove the insulation from about 1 inch (2.5 cm) at the ends of both wire pieces. It works best to

gently cut into the plastic covering and then pull it away with your fingernails. Be careful not to cut through the wires. Twist one end of each wire tightly around each fastener head. Press the fastener heads firmly against the cardboard and spread their prongs apart on the other side of the cardboard. This will be the switch.

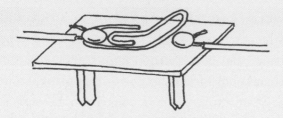

TO OPEN AN ELECTRIC CURRENT
Attach the battery clip to the points on the top of the battery. Attach the loose ends of the switch wires to the battery clip wires by wrapping them around the battery clip wires. Slide the compass to sit under one of the wires, with the compass needle and wire pointed in the same direction. You'll notice that the compass needle is pointing north. Turn the electric current on by pressing down on the paper clip. The electric current stored in the battery flows through the wire, into the brass paper fastener, and through the paper clip. It's a complete circle, as the current flows out of one bat-

tery terminal, through the wiring and switch, then back into the other battery terminal.

As the current flows, watch what it does to the compass needle. You may also notice the paper clip getting hot because the electricity is moving the atoms so quickly that they heat up. Keep the switch on for only three seconds at a time to preserve the battery and to keep the wire from heating up.

What happened? You turned on an electric current, which created a different magnetic field. The wire's magnetic field isn't as strong as the earth's, so this only works when you place a compass very close to the wire. When the current is turned off, the compass returns to pointing toward earth's magnetic North Pole.

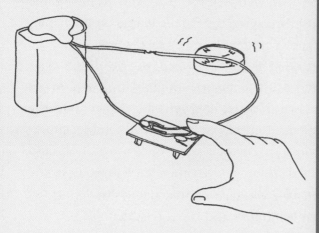

Tom because it not only paid well, it also gave him a chance to practice writing quickly so he could get faster at taking telegraph messages. He taught himself to write in an efficient, quick way, making his letters small and straight because it was faster to write that way when taking down messages. Years later, Thomas Edison invented a copying machine, called the mimeograph, which could make multiple copies from one master. His job as a hand-copyist helped him recognize the need for such a timesaving invention.

Tom's copying speed improved immensely. He was soon winning intercity tournaments in which telegraph operators competed to see who could write down incoming messages the fastest. Tom moved from city to city, living in Cincinnati, Ohio, and Indianapolis, Indiana. When the Civil War ended in 1865, Tom moved to Nashville, then Memphis, Tennessee, then on to Louisville, Kentucky. Because the South was still under military occupation by Union army forces, telegraphers could easily find work there for the military.

Tom stayed in Louisville for a year, working for Western Union, saving his money to collect books and lab equipment.

Head East, Young Man

In 1867, at age 20, Tom went home to Port Huron to visit his parents and discovered that his beloved mother was ill from depression and mental stress. The family home had been taken over by the military due to an expansion of the facility at Fort Gratiot, and the Edisons were renting a small place until they could find something else. They were penniless, and Tom's mother had difficulty dealing with the setbacks. His father was unable to cope as well and spent little time at home. Tom stayed a while, helping the family with money, but decided he couldn't stay home for good. He wrote to a friend, who encouraged him to move to Boston, where a Western Union office was hiring. After doing some work repairing electrical cable for the Grand Trunk Railroad, Tom received a free rail pass to Boston, and he made the 1,000-mile (1,609-km) trip.

In a time when newspaper editors encouraged young men to "go West" for success, Thomas Edison headed east instead, in particular because Boston was the center of electrical science at the time. He arrived at the Western Union office in a disheveled state, his hair and clothes rumpled from the long trip. Nonetheless, after conducting a five-minute interview and seeing a sample of his hand-writing, the manager hired Tom to begin as a telegrapher that same evening.

To the polished Boston telegraphers, Tom was a wild character, and they didn't believe anyone who looked and acted so rough could be as good a telegraph operator as he claimed. His coworkers set him up to receive messages from the fastest sender in New York, whose reputation was known to all except Tom. The New Yorker began sending the copy slowly, then increased until the speed was very fast. Tom, realizing something was going on because the Boston coworkers were all standing around, watching and smiling, kept pace easily. Then he began to embellish his act, stopping to sharpen his pencil, and then catching right up. Finally, he broke into the wire and sent a message back to the speedy New Yorker, telling him "say, young man, change off and send with the other foot." That made the New York man angry, and he quit sending. The Boston crew realized that Tom truly did know how to do the job, and do it well. After that, Tom impressed his colleagues with a few tricks, such as his homemade electrical cockroach paralyzer, and they became friends.

For Tom, however, moving to Boston meant more than simply showing off his telegraphy skills. He had mastered the telegraph and wanted new challenges. Just writing down messages quickly bored him. He was curious about how electricity made the telegraph work, and he always tried to find ways to improve and expand the ability of the telegraph to send messages instantly. It worked because of electricity, something very few people understood in the 1860s. Tom realized he would have to teach himself, so he got a copy of the book *Experimental Researches in Electricity,* by Michael Faraday, and began studying electricity.

Edison read Faraday's important work with interest, trying out all the experiments on his own. He told a friend, "I'm now 21. I may live to be 50. Can I get as much done as he did? I have got so much to do and life is so short, I am going to hustle." And hustle he did. He set out to improve the telegraph, to allow it to send more than one message down the wire at a time. He was so excited about the idea, his roommate in the boardinghouse described Edison as working like his "brain was on fire."

Tom Edison jumped wholeheartedly into trying to improve the telegraph and created a rough system that would send two messages on one wire at once. He called it a duplex telegraph and inserted stories in the Boston newspaper announcing he was setting up shop as an independent inventor and would be selling the item soon. With that, he quit his job at Western Union and went into the invention business—with no money and an invention that might not really work.

Edison needed to find some way to finance his business. He found an investor who gave him $500 to get started, in exchange for a share of the profits once the duplex telegraph was marketed. He had another idea, too—to create a vote-recording machine, and he found an investor who gave him a hundred dollars to create it. Edison was in business!

Vote-Recording Machine

The electric vote-recording machine was an instant success—at least in Edison's eyes. It was his first patented idea (see sidebar on page 41), filed in the U.S. Patent Office in Washington, DC, on October 6, 1868. It was a simple machine that recorded votes using electromagnetic impulses. He thought it would save a lot of time in Congress, where voting seemed to take forever. He made the first model out of wood, with wires running from the machine to the desks of the voters, where they were connected to two buttons, one for Yea and one for Nay. When the voter pressed a button, the impulse traveled through the wire to the machine, where it was

recorded with a number. Just a glance at the machine would tell how many votes had been cast for either decision.

Edison thought it would be easy to sell the system to every state legislature (there were 37 states at that time) as well as to the U.S. Con-

MICHAEL FARADAY

|||||||||||||||||||||||||||||||||| (1791–1867) ||||||||||||||||||||||||||||||||||||

MICHAEL FARADAY was a British scientist who studied the relationship between electricity and magnetism, discovering the phenomenon called electromagnetic induction: the production of electric current by a change in magnetic intensity. He demonstrated how it worked by wrapping a wire around an iron ring, with ends connected to the terminals of a battery. The wrapped wire caused an electromagnetic field to build up, due to the movement of electricity through the wires.

Faraday was a hero for many young people in the 19th century because he had been a poor boy who went to work as an apprentice to a bookseller. While working, he read as much as possible and began doing his own experiments. Eventually he was hired to work as an assistant to the famous English scientist Humphrey Davy, who was also working on the foundations of electrical theory.

Faraday was successful at creating several innovations that made working with electricity possible, including the first dynamo and an electric motor. He is known as the "Father of Electricity."

Michael Faraday's book *Experimental Researches in Electricity* is available to read online or download to a computer at the Project Gutenberg Web site: www.Gutenberg.org (search for "Michael Faraday").

North Wind Picture Archives

gress. He figured it would bring him at least $50,000. Not so. The Massachusetts state legislature passed on it, saying it wouldn't allow members to filibuster—to discuss and debate as they voted. Edison trudged to Washington, DC, to try his luck there, but he got the same response. The congressman who listened to Edison's sales pitch for the machine told him, "Young man, that is just what we do *not* want. Your invention would destroy the only hope that the minority would have of influencing legislation." Chagrined, Edison learned a big lesson he never forgot the rest of his life. He decided he would only work on inventions that could be widely sold to everyone.

A Pair of Inventions

Tom turned back to the workshop, creating an improved stock ticker device to record the changing price of gold stocks. The financial markets were growing in the years after the Civil War, and stock traders, investors, and bankers needed to know the changing price information. Edison's device was an improvement over the others on the market and brought him a second patent as well as a new investor. The machine used electrical current and electromagnets to receive signals that were printed out on a piece of paper tape.

Subscribers paid for the service and had wires run from their stock tickers to the main one in Edison's office. Other types of electrical devices were connected to a central system with wires, too, such as telegraphs, burglar alarms, and fire alarm systems. Wires connecting different systems were tacked up to roofs and poles all over Boston, New York, and other cities where the new services were available to subscribers.

Edison also set to work on perfecting the duplex telegraph system he had announced earlier. Others had been trying for years to send more than one message over the telegraph wire at the same time, because it would double, or even triple, telegraph profits, depending upon the number of messages that could be sent. As it was, outgoing messages piled up at the telegraph office, and most were sent at night when the lines were more often open. There was a great need for a duplex system, and Edison figured it would be the perfect invention to launch his stalled career as an inventor.

He finally learned how to make a duplex system and set out to test it with a telegraph company in New York City (the Western Union office in Boston had no interest in his idea). He set off for Rochester, New York, with a load of equipment and paraphernalia, and contacted a New York telegrapher who would be seated at the opposite end of his special system. When the big test came, it didn't work. Either the other telegrapher didn't understand how to respond to the duplex, or the system malfunctioned. Edison went back to Boston in dismay, embarrassment, and frustration. He was completely broke, had no investors left, and no idea what to do next.

Edison invented a stock ticker that operated like a telegraph to send prices quickly over wires.

Success in New York City

Feeling he had no future in Boston, Tom stored his equipment and tools and left for New York City, without a cent in his pocket. At age 22, he did have a brilliant mind and knowledge about electricity, circuits, magnetism, and technology that few others could match. He also had plenty of courage. He had only one friend in New York, and when he arrived on that friend's doorstep to spend the night, no one was home. Edison spent the night walking the streets, because he had no money for a room.

He searched around for anyone who might help him get started in the city and found a fellow at the Gold Indicator Company who had purchased one of his stock ticker machines. The man liked Edison's work, so he let him sleep on a cot in the room where the company's battery was stored and work on experiments in the machine shop until he found a job.

Not long afterward, the Gold Indicator Company's main stock ticker machine broke down. The business was threatened with collapse until Tom was able get it functioning again with a few simple repairs. The business owner hired him at a hefty salary, and Tom was secure, able to continue refining and working on telegraph inventions. But soon, the business owner sold out to Western Union, and Tom was faced with either working for Western Union again, or quitting. He decided it was time to set out as an independent inventor again.

This time he had a partner, the fellow who had originally allowed him to sleep in the Gold Indicator Company's basement, Franklin Pope, who was also an electrical engineer. The two placed an advertisement in the newspaper and announced they were in business to build electrical devices and equipment, set up private telegraph lines, or create scientific equipment on order. Edison lived with Pope and his wife, but spent most of his time in the Pope, Edison, & Company workshop.

The new business was a success. In a short time, Edison was sending money home to help his parents and had filed for seven patents covering a range of new projects. When the company began building an improved stock quotation machine Edison had designed, the Western Union Company promptly bought the rights to the idea to keep it off the market because it threatened Western Union's own machine and the monopoly it had in the market. Western Union paid $15,000 to keep the machine from being manufactured, which was a welcome amount of funds for the two inventors.

Western Union had become a huge company after the Civil War. Its telegraph lines spanned the continent, and when smaller companies grew up to compete, Western Union bought them to eliminate rivalry. The company hired teams of inventors to work on new projects, too. One of the managers at Western Union had said, "Edison is a genius and a very fiend for work." Western Union quickly hired him to invent for them, too. A regular salary and the chance to spend all day inventing were too good to resist; Edison ended his business partnership with Franklin Pope and began working for Western Union.

A device that improved the stock ticker was so important to Western Union that the company offered to pay Edison $40,000 for the patent. He nearly fell over when they told him the amount. He had never had much money and thought it was a real fortune. He signed a contract, which he didn't understand at all, and pocketed the check. Just like anyone who had never handled much money, he had no idea what to do with a check. Not many people used checks in the 1870s, and certainly not Thomas Edison. He went to the nearby bank—he'd never been inside a bank before—and went to a teller's window. He couldn't understand what they said (due to his deafness) and walked away crestfallen. The piece of paper was worthless, he believed. The teller wouldn't even give him 10 dollars for it. It had all been a mean trick.

He went back to the Western Union offices, where the staff teased him. The teller had insisted on identification for such a large amount of cash, but Edison had no idea what he meant. This time, someone from Western Union went back to the bank with him, and the teller handed over a pile of 10- and 20-dollar bills. The cash was a huge pile, about a foot high. Edison took it home and stuffed it in his clothing and under the bed. He sat up all night in his New Jersey boardinghouse room, afraid he would be murdered because he had so much cash. Friends advised him to get a bank account, so he took the money back to the bank and gave it back, in exchange for a little book that recorded the amount of money he had in the bank.

It was time for Tom Edison to start thinking like a businessperson.

Thomas Edison poses with his favorite invention, the phonograph, at age 33.

U.S. Dept. of the Interior, National Park Service, Edison National Historic Site

4

Getting Down to Business

> "MY DESIRE IS TO DO EVERYTHING WITHIN MY POWER TO FURTHER FREE THE PEOPLE FROM DRUDGERY AND CREATE THE LARGEST POSSIBLE MEASURES OF HAPPINESS AND PROSPERITY."
> —THOMAS EDISON

Inventing Becomes a Career

IN THE WINTER of 1871, 24-year-old Thomas Edison started his own invention and manufacturing business. Western Union had ordered 1,200 stock ticker machines, for a total of nearly half a million dollars, to be delivered over the next few years. It was a clear signal he would be a success. Edison scoured the area for a good location and found a spot on the top floor of a three-story building in Newark, New Jersey. He purchased a lot of machinery and began hiring employees. Within a month, he had spent all the money he'd made from the sale of his stock ticker patent to equip the new venture. He initially worked with business partners, such as William Unger,

George Harrington, Joseph Murray, and others, but the partnerships faded as Edison's own financial situation improved and he could finance his ideas himself.

Edison was elated about the way life was going, except for concerns about his parents. He sent them money but was sad to hear his mother's health was failing. By spring, she had died. He went back home by train to attend the funeral and burial, but he didn't stay.

He was soon back in Newark, embarking on a great period in his life. He hired enthusiastic young workers who knew little more about electricity than he did, and together they figured out how to make machines or solve problems no one else had solved before. Edison was very young to be running such an enterprise, yet his workers teasingly called him the "old man." He had a desk in one corner and would create an invention, jump up and wildly dance around if it worked, then give it to his craftsmen to copy. Edison worked long hours and expected his employees to do the same. To reward them and keep them interested in their work, he made bets with them or offered prizes. If something turned out especially well, he would call for a holiday and take everyone on a fishing excursion.

As a business manager, Edison had his own methods. He kept no records of accounts, of purchases or payments, or statements due.

He only kept payroll records so he would know how much to pay the employees. All other papers he stuffed into a drawer. He waited to pay a bill until the second or third request, and then he hustled around for the money. "This saved the humbuggery of bookkeeping, which I never understood," he admitted. He didn't like bookkeepers because he had once hired one who made a huge mistake, telling him there was $7,500 left after expenses. Edison was overjoyed at having more profits than expected and planned a big party for all the employees. But, looking over the records the night before the party, he discovered the bookkeeper hadn't included some large expenses. There weren't any big profits. He cancelled the party, swallowed his pride, and fired the bookkeeper.

At the Newark workshop, he set aside a small laboratory area for himself, where he could continue his beloved experiments. In 1871 he began keeping notebook records of his experiments (see sidebar at right), jotting down the materials he used and the results. On the first page of the notebook, he wrote:

"This will be a daily record containing ideas previously formed, some of which have been tried, some that have been sketched and described, and some that have never been sketched, tried, or described."

The first work he turned to was the duplex telegraph, which he had never truly perfected. He jotted in the notebook, "Invented by & for myself and not for any small-brained capitalist." It's interesting that Edison felt that way about the financiers he depended upon for funding, because by that time his successful stock ticker machine was helping capitalists around the world keep track of wealth, investments, and gains.

Edison Starts a Family

By 1871, Thomas Edison was undeniably successful. He had established a profitable business and made connections with investors and promoters. Yet, his personal life was lacking. Still a very young man of 24, he continued to live in a boardinghouse room and had not taken the time to court young women, least of all settle down into marriage and family life. His father, back in Michigan, had remarried, to a 16-year-old neighbor. Tom's new stepmother was far younger than himself! Tom, who had always been shy around girls, fell in love with one of the young women working in his shop. Several women worked for Edison in various jobs; at that time they were punching dots and dashes by hand onto paper tape to be sent through the automatic telegraph.

One teenager, 16-year-old Mary Stilwell, fascinated Tom. She was a local girl from a poor family, a tall blonde who was shy, yet friendly with everyone on the staff.

Tom was in love, but he didn't quite know how to proceed. An awkward suitor, he spent most of his time watching Mary work, not knowing what to say to start conversation. She would become nervous as her boss stood and watched her work, until at times she couldn't continue punching the tapes.

At one point, Tom said to her, "What do you think of me . . . do you like me?"

She was surprised and didn't know how to respond. "Don't be in a hurry about telling me," he continued. "It doesn't matter much, unless you would like to marry me."

She stammered, not knowing how to respond to such a proposal. He went on, "Think it over, talk to your mother about it, and let me know as soon as convenient; Tuesday, say. Next week, Tuesday, I mean."

The awkward proposal was over.

Mary thought about it, and the two began a courtship that involved Tom and a friend escorting Mary and her sister to church, along with visits in the Stilwell family's parlor. While seated quietly in the parlor, Tom and Mary "chatted" with each other using Morse code, tapping messages with their fingers on each other's palm. They were married a few weeks later, on Christmas Day, 1871. After the ceremony and lunch, the new Mr. and Mrs. Edison moved into a comfortable home in Newark that Tom had purchased the week before.

Their first child, daughter Marion, was born a year later, and they nicknamed her "Dot," after the Morse code. When a son, Thomas junior, was born in 1876, they called him "Dash." Their third child, William Leslie, was born two years later.

Mary was a perfect wife for Tom; she didn't interfere with his work and kept the home running smoothly. She didn't get along with his father, however, and when Tom invited him to come stay with them, he wrote, "My wife does not, nor never can, control me. . . ." She certainly didn't. He spent most evenings, sometimes days in a row, at the workshop, while she and the children stayed at home. Mary's younger sister, Alice, moved in and stayed for several years before she got married, to keep Mary company. Mary was frequently lonely and bored. Being married to Thomas Edison was not easy.

Tom rarely spent time with his family except on Sundays. He loved Mary and the children, but they didn't fit into his world of invention. He was dismayed that Mary, whom he fondly called "Popsy-Wopsy," wasn't interested in inventing things, too. He had few hobbies or interests besides work, and according to Dot, "father's work always came first."

Ups and Downs

In 1872, Edison patented 38 new ideas or improvements on prior inventions, and in 1873 another 25 patents. Not every patent was for a completely unique project, because patent laws also protect minor improvements and changes to existing ideas.

In order to come up with new ideas, Edison had to know everything about inventions that had already been devised, how they worked, and what their weaknesses might be. Then he could identify potential solutions. This took a tremendous amount of research, which Edison thrived on. A visitor described one instance when Edison ordered a pile of chemistry books stacked five feet high, stayed at his desk night and day, eating at the desk and sleeping in the chair, until after six weeks he had read them all, made notes, tried 2,000 experiments, and found a solution to the problem he was working on.

The Automatic Telegraph Company hired Edison to perfect the telegraph machine, and he was able to redesign it to send messages at speeds of up to 1,000 words a minute, which were received by machines that embossed the messages on paper, creating an automatic telegraph that didn't rely as much on operators to send and transmit messages.

In 1873 a financial depression swept the nation, and many businesses went bankrupt. Edison and his business partners struggled to keep the workshops open, but even paying the taxes was difficult. Rather than close up shop, Edison turned to inventions, working feverishly to come up with a wide range of devices he thought might bring in some money.

The workshops and labs patented several new products, including paraffin paper (sold as waxed paper today). Edison found that giving paper a coating of wax made it easy to press or cut the paper into stencils. That led to inventing the mimeograph machine, a forerunner of today's copy machine. The mimeograph used waxed-paper "masters" that could be inscribed with the text to be copied. In those days, there weren't any typewriters, so the words could be inscribed with a steel-tipped pen or by pressing the master against a page of metal type used in printing. After giving the master a light coat of ink, the indentions in the wax would hold enough ink to make several copies when paper was pressed against it. Fastening the master to a cylinder with a handle for turning made it possible to "crank out" multiple copies. The mimeograph was a very useful invention that

PATENTS AND COPYRIGHTS

A PATENT gives an inventor the right to produce his or her invented product without allowing others to copy it. Patents protect inventors, and, because a patent may be sold by the owner to others who want to manufacture the item, patents create value in an invention.

The U.S. Constitution provides for patent protection. Patent protection gives people a reason to try to invent things, because they can make a living or even become rich from their ideas. Patent protection lasts for 20 years. After that, the idea becomes "public domain," and anyone else can make and sell the item. Generic prescription drugs are an example of copycat manufacturing after a medicine's patent has expired.

While it may not seem fair to everyone, the idea of public domain was put in the Constitution to prevent monopolies from taking control of inventions everyone needed. Inventors can make as much money as possible with their new idea during the first 20 years. After that, they can improve the product and patent the improvements or compete with others who can use their idea to make products, too.

A patent application must be filed with the U.S. Patent Office in Washington, DC. There are three types of patents:

- **Utility patent**—protects an invention, machine, or improvement on a previous invention
- **Design patent**—protects the way something looks or is designed
- **Plant patent**—granted to anyone who invents or discovers and grows any new variety of plant

Every country has its own patent laws. A group of 140 countries joined the Paris Convention for the Protection of Industrial Property, a treaty between countries that honors patents. But not every country in the world belongs to the group or agrees to protect foreign patents.

A copyright is different from a patent. A patent protects inventors, while a copyright protects artists, composers, authors, and others from having their work copied.

remained popular in offices until the 1970s, when photocopy machines became available.

Thomas Edison no doubt understood the importance of making quick, simple copies—after all, he'd earned money years before as a copyist, handwriting plays. Edison sold the mimeograph patent to A. B. Dick, for a small amount of money, however, and didn't receive the fortune it eventually earned.

Thinking along the lines of making communication more efficient, Edison also invented the electric pen. It was a clever device that used a small motor on top of the pen, connected by wires to two batteries. The motor powered a needle up and down at the tip of the pen. It would perforate tiny holes in a sheet of paper, dropping a tiny bit of ink into each one. Copies of the original document written with the pen could be made by pressing blank paper against the original—the little dots of ink imprinted on the copy. To help sales, Edison even gave public demonstrations using the pen. While today it seems awkward and unwieldy, the electric pen was a huge success, with 60,000 sold to government and business offices.

While the electric pen remained popular for a while, it was replaced by other inventions such as carbon paper and, eventually, photocopiers. Another offshoot idea came from the pen, however, and that was the tattoo machine. Today, tattoos are made using devices similar to Thomas Edison's original electric pen, etching colored inks into tiny holes poked in the skin.

Pens, waxed paper, and even mimeographs were OK, but they weren't the sort of "big" inventions Thomas Edison dreamed of making. He'd made plenty of small inventions, receiving more than 200 patents in the seven years since he went to New York to begin an invention career. He'd been able to keep his business afloat during hard times, but money wasn't flowing in. And he wasn't getting much fame for inventing little—though useful—machines. He wanted something more, something really important.

The telegraph remained his big challenge. He still wanted to create a way to send more than one message over the wire at once. An English inventor had created a system in which two messages could be sent at once, but in opposite directions. Edison wanted to send them the same direction. He had been working on this for years when it occurred to him that if he could send two messages in each direction, he would be sending four at once. The idea continued to tantalize him. In one of his lab notebooks he drew a design called "Fourplex No. 14" and the words "Why not?" Somehow he would meet the challenge.

Problems with financing remained. The Western Union Company's stock was falling, and the company was reluctant to give Edi-

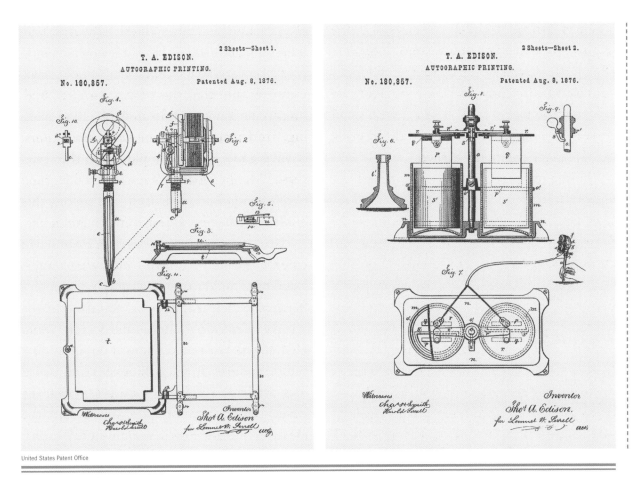

The patent drawings for Edison's electric pen. Drawings of an invention have to be filed with the U.S. Patent Office, so the invention can be clearly understood by anyone.

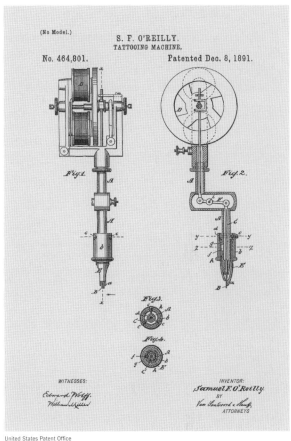

This drawing is of S. F. O'Reilly's invention, the tattoo machine, which clearly resembles Edison's electric pen. It's an example of how one idea sparks another.

son money to perfect the four-way quadruplex device, so he went to another firm, a smaller rival telegraph company. It was funded by magnate Jay Gould, a financier who had tried to capture the nation's gold supply with a financial scheme a few years earlier.

Gould owned railroads and banks, and was one of the era's "robber barons"—wealthy men who created monopolies (and fortunes) in the new industries after the Civil War.

After the 1873 depression, Jay Gould ended up owning many of the nation's rail-

MAKE COPIES WITH A STENCIL

UNTIL EDISON invented the mimeograph, people made copies by using stencils. Edison attached a stencil to a cylinder that could be turned around and around to make several copies. Try this activity to see how stencils can be used to make a copy of an original.

YOU'LL NEED

* Ink pen or felt marker
* 3 or 4 pieces of drawing paper, any size
* Acetate sheet (available at art supply stores) or other sheet of stiff, clear plastic, such as from a page protector or photo album
* Scissors
* Tape or 4 paper clips
* Sponges
* Poster paint in several colors

Sketch out a simple design made up of shapes—triangles, squares, circles—leaving space between them. Then draw your design on the plastic. Cut the shapes out of the plastic sheet; this is your stencil. Place the stencil on a sheet of plain paper, either taping it in place or using paper clips around the edges to hold it in place. You don't want it to move or smudge as you work. You're ready to make a print.

Dip the sponge in paint, then squeeze it almost dry so the paint doesn't drip. Use the sponge to dab paint onto the stencil, allowing the paint to color the paper behind the openings. Lift the stencil carefully and position it on another sheet of paper to make a second copy. You can continue making copies of the same design, which are called "prints."

Get creative. Use several different designs and different colors (use a separate sponge for each color). Try overlapping designs, or adding details with a pen when the paint is dry. You can make a set of holiday cards, all with the same original design.

roads, banks, and newspapers, as well as some telegraph companies. He put his own companies' telegraph wires alongside his rail tracks, covering much of the nation. Gould's telegraph companies were still smaller than Western Union, but they were indeed competitors. It wasn't long before Gould decided to purchase Thomas Edison's improved telegraph patents and use them to build a company that could put Western Union out of business.

Using the automatic telegraph Edison had invented (which Western Union wasn't interested in), Gould and his telegraph companies began the "telegraphic war" to take over the telegraph market in the United States. Gould challenged Western Union to compete in a public contest, during which an 11,130-word message by President Grant was sent over the wires. Edison's automatic system sent the message the quickest, in 60 minutes; Western Union came in 10 minutes later.

Thomas Edison still wanted to make a quadruplex telegraph system. Having worked with Western Union in the past, he went to the company for money to begin developing it. He set up shop in the company's basement, working around the clock to create a quadruplex system that could send four messages in two directions at once. Edison used an ingenious system of circuits, condensers, batteries, relays, and other devices to send two messages over the same wire at the same time. The two messages went at different electrical frequencies, and the automatic receivers at each end picked up only the message sent at their frequency. It was very complicated, and in order to understand how it worked, Edison built himself a model using tubes filled with water, moving the water through a system of pipes and valves as if it were electrical pulses. Those who saw him at the time claimed he didn't eat or sleep regularly for a week—he just grabbed coffee and cake from a café and slept in a chair from time to time. He used to say that napping while working gave him a chance to dream about solutions to his project.

In no time, he had a working quadruplex, tested it out, and was ready to patent it. Then George Prescott, the chief engineer at Western Union, told him the company wouldn't pay Edison unless Prescott was named as co-inventor and got half the profits. Edison was desperate for money—he owed $10,000 on his house in Newark—so he agreed. But Western Union didn't come up with the payment. However, Gould's Atlantic and Pacific Telegraph Company needed a few inventions, so he worked out some products for them and was able to keep his house.

Western Union kept dragging out payment, so Edison sold his share of the quadru-

plex patent to Gould's Atlantic and Pacific Telegraph Company. Now Gould's company owned half of the invention and Western Union owned half, and they spent years battling over the rights to the quadruplex in court, often calling Edison in as witness. The newspapers covered the telegraph war between the two companies, as well as information about Edison's valuable invention. It made him famous, although he was only 27 years old. The quadruplex saved telegraph companies over $20 million dollars over the next 30 years.

When Edison sold his share to Gould, Gould promised him 10 percent of the profits from the quadruplex as well as a steady job with another of Gould's companies, the Automatic Telegraph Company. But Gould didn't

RECEIVER
MAIN LINES
GROUND
MAIN BATTERIES
N P N P
TRANSMITTER
GROUND

Edison: His Life and Inventions, Harper Brothers, 1910

This drawing shows Edison's quadruplex, which could send messages over four telegraph wires at once, greatly improving the telegraph. Before the quadruplex, operators had to wait for an open line to send a message.

keep his promises. Two years later, Edison went back to freelance inventing for Western Union. In 1881, the Atlantic and Pacific Telegraph Company and Western Union merged stock, and Gould took over both companies. Thomas Edison knew he would have no future continuing to invent for the telegraph industry. "When Gould got the Western Union," he said, "I knew no further progress in telegraphy was possible, and I went into other lines."

Invention Factory

Thomas Edison began moving into other types of work while inventing for Western Union. He knew he needed a large, private place to do all the work he planned, one that couldn't be taken from him if he ran out of money. In 1874, Thomas Edison's father, Samuel, had moved to New Jersey to be near his son and grandchildren. Although he'd worried that his son wouldn't amount to much because of his unruly behavior as a child, Samuel was very proud of his son's success. People said he was so proud of Tom it was almost embarrassing. He was able to assist Tom with a big step forward in his business career. Thomas Edison decided to build a research factory—the first of its kind in the world. He and his employees would turn out practical inventions on a regular schedule. It was almost an invention itself, as no one had done anything like it before, relying on luck or happy accidents to create new inventions.

There were some scientific laboratories at universities and the Smithsonian Institution, but they were just for research. Edison wanted inventions. He promised the new lab would turn out "a minor invention every 10 days and a big thing every six months or so." He would also test, improve, and perfect other inventors' work for a fee.

Thomas and Samuel began hiring builders for construction of the world's first commercial research laboratory in Menlo Park, New Jersey. Today, many companies own research labs where they search for new and better products, but in the 1870s no one else had begun such a thing. Edison built his workshop and laboratory in the small village about 25 miles from New York City because it was close enough to do business in the city but far enough away from the congestion and pollution. It was a quiet country setting, with railroads running nearby, where Edison and his staff could enjoy a quiet life, devote themselves to their work, and avoid the prying eyes of competitors. Sometimes legal patent protection wasn't enough. Industrial spies were often sent to apply for jobs at Edison's labs or to tour the labs as visitors, hoping to see some new idea or invention they could tell his competitors about. The security guards at Edison's lab took their job seriously. One new security guard wouldn't let Thomas Edison himself into the front gate without identification!

The compound consisted of a huge barn-like building that had partitions for a small office, a library, and a drawing room on the ground floor, with workshop space on the second floor. The second floor was one long room filled with tables full of instruments, batteries, and equipment. The walls held shelves full of chemicals in jars, and bins of supplies and materials like wire, wax, rubber, and pieces of metals. At first, just over a dozen men worked there, and they rented rooms in a boardinghouse down the road.

Menlo Park became famous as a "Science Village," where smart and dedicated workers

INVENT SOMETHING!

SEE IF YOU can come up with an object that does something in a new way. An improved mousetrap? An ice cream scoop machine? A cat watering dish? Think about things you might use around your house, then try to come up with a new way to do it. Someone just patented Shower Scrubbies—thongs for your feet with brushes on the soles, so you can scrub your shower by dancing around under the water spray.

Once you have your idea, you may want to apply for a patent to protect it from copycats. You don't need a finished product to apply for a patent;

Thomas Edison often submitted patent applications based on an just an idea.

YOU'LL NEED

❋ Black pen
❋ Sketch pad of white paper

Complete information about patents and how to apply for them is on the U.S. Patent Office Web site: www.uspto.gov. Here are the basics.

First make sure that no one else has already patented your invention. Look in catalogs, stores,

and online. Make a clear drawing of your invention in black ink, on white paper. You may need several drawings at different angles. Make as many as needed to show how your invention is built.

Write a description of how the invention works and a description of the drawing. If you are under 18 years old, you're considered a legal minor, so your parent or guardian must apply for the patent for you. Getting and keeping a patent is expensive. It costs $790 to file an application, $1,370 when the patent is issued, and $6,410 to maintain the patent during the next $11\frac{1}{2}$ years.

invented, improved, and produced products that nearly everyone eventually used. Edison's staff included mathematicians, glass blowers, carpenters, scientists, and many other types of tradesmen. One thing they all had in common was that they worked hard. When young William Hammer applied for a job, Edison told him that most applicants "only wanted to know two things: how much we pay and how long we work. Well, we don't pay anything and we work all the time." Hammer eagerly accepted a job and stayed on for years. Contrary to Edison's claim that "we don't pay anything," he paid his employees fairly, in fact more than other employers did, and gave them extra pay and royalty rights to certain products they created. Most importantly, they were given ideas to work on, plenty of supplies, and freedom to come up with solutions on their own while working as part of a team.

Edison's staff adored him. One of his employees, Robert Halgrim, said, "He was always playing practical jokes on everyone in the lab. You could pull one on him if you were good enough. It was his wonderful personality that kept one working for him, to realize that he was working harder than anyone else." Everyone worked long hours without complaint and looked at Edison as a hero. When it was vital for work to go on all night, which often happened because of a deadline, Edison had meals brought in and put a large pipe organ in the laboratory so people could play for sing-alongs during long stretches of work. These midnight suppers were fun, and the workers returned to their tasks refreshed after a meal and entertainment.

Edison himself worked night and day and was able to fall asleep anywhere. He took naps

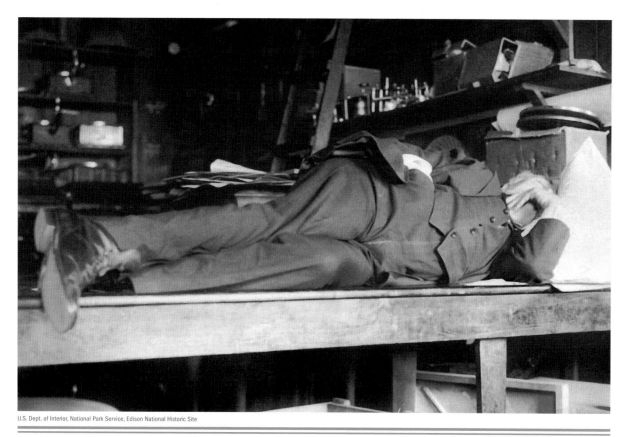

U.S. Dept. of Interior, National Park Service, Edison National Historic Site

Edison could take a nap anywhere—here he's dozing in the workshop.

in the corner of the laboratory on a cot or in a chair, sometimes with his head propped on a thick chemical dictionary. His staff joked that he absorbed the knowledge out of the dictionary during his sleep. Edison knew he was able to fall asleep nearly anywhere because he was nearly deaf—noise around him didn't awaken him because he couldn't hear it.

These years at Menlo Park, with his young family and growing laboratory facility, were happy ones. Successes from some inventions gave him the money and freedom to choose and work on whatever projects he wanted. Wealthy men from New York began fighting to get his patents, paying him well for rights to produce what he and his workers invented.

And the inventions seemed to flow out in a stream: devices to improve telegraph and ocean cables, electric writing pens, mimeographs, sound measuring instruments, and information about many chemicals and drugs.

National Library of Medicine

Inside Edison's chemical laboratory.

Making a Telephone That Worked

Several inventors had been working on a telephonelike device to send sound over telegraph cables, but nothing worked well enough to be widely used. The most famous telephone inventor was Alexander Graham Bell (see sidebar on page 50), the first to patent a working telephone. But the first telephones didn't work very well. People spoke through and listened from the same opening. Voices weren't very clear. Worst of all, the early telephones only worked over a very short distance.

The Western Union Company knew the telephone would eventually replace the telegraph, and it wanted to get in on the

ALEXANDER GRAHAM BELL

||||||||||||||||||||||||||||||||||| (1847–1922) |||||||||||||||||||||||||||||||||||||||

ALEXANDER BELL was born in Scotland. He added the name Graham later, because he admired a family friend by that name. His father, grandfather, and uncle taught speech therapy and public speaking. His mother was deaf, and that spurred him to invent a device that could create sounds that she could hear. He developed a piano that transmitted music over electrical wires. When Bell was 25 years old he opened a school in Boston to train teachers to work with students who were deaf. He taught lipreading—reading other people's statements by watching the movement of their mouth as they speak—which he termed "visible speech."

In the 1870s many inventors worked to create a machine that would transmit or record the human voice. Bell worked with Thomas Watson on telegraph and telephone technology, becoming the first to patent a telephone, in 1876. Eventually, Bell registered 18 patents for inventions and shared another 12 with collaborators.

On the day Alexander Graham Bell filed his patent for the telephone, another inventor, Elisha Gray, filed a similar patent two hours later. Gray had been working on the telephone for years but hadn't patented his ideas. Bell perfected Gray's ideas, as well as ideas shown at the Philadelphia Exhibition of 1884 by Antonio Meucci, who didn't patent his ideas early, either. There were many people working on perfecting a speaking machine, but Bell was the first to patent, and the first to set up a company to market the machine, the Bell Telephone Company.

Bell also invented the first metal detector. In his later years, Bell created devices for airplanes, such as the aileron, a hinged piece attached to an airplane's wing that can be moved by the pilot in order to control the rising and falling, or roll, of the plane in the air.

Library of Congress, LC-USZ62-3205

telephone industry in the beginning. But before it could become an industry, someone had to figure out how to make the telephone work better. Western Union turned to the inventor it knew best: Thomas Edison. He had worked for the company as a young telegrapher and later as an inventor and manufacturer of improved telegraph equipment. He seemed the perfect choice to come up with a better way to send human voices, instead of electric dots and dashes, over the wires.

Edison had already been working on a similar project, so he agreed to improve Bell's telephone by adding his own ideas for a microphone that sent voice signals better. He was hard at work on the electric light bulb, and had been using carbon, a substance his workers collected by burning candles inside glass globes. The black sticky stuff that collected on the inside of the glass was carbon, and Edison scraped it off and rolled it into a button shape, creating an excellent voice transmitter inside the telephone.

Edison's carbon button worked better than anything anyone else had tried. It was placed between two metal plates, which were connected to a battery circuit and to the diaphragm. Carbon was the key, because when pressure was applied to it, it changed its electrical resistance. Edison had used carbon in his quadruplex to raise or lower pressure in order to create varying conductivity over the telegraph line. Now, with the carbon button pressed tightly against the metal plates, vibrations from the human voice would cause the carbon to send impulses over the electrically charged wire. It was the microphone that made the voice sound loud and crisp—a big improvement over Bell's telephone with its weak and garbled sounds.

The first time Edison tested it, his telephone worked over a distance of 106 miles, between Philadelphia and New York City. The carbon button transmitter improved Bell's telephone so much that Edison patented it himself. The carbon transmitter made the telephone truly practical and was used in radio broadcasting, too.

Western Union snapped up Edison's patent, paying him $100,000 for the rights. He knew if he were paid the huge sum of money at once he'd spend all of it on research and supplies, so he asked for payments over six years, giving him a stable source of income as he plunged into other work.

The telephone might have remained a novelty if Edison hadn't worked out the problems so it actually functioned as a communication tool. With a few more innovations, the telephone was truly successful, and it would be decades before there were any more improvements to the telephone. Meanwhile, Edison enjoyed the telephone as much as anyone. He had one installed in the laboratory and often called his wife at home in the evening, telling her to "send lunch down for seven—we'll be working all night."

Thomas Edison worked on communication tools, such as the telegraph and telephone, that allowed people to talk to each other, but he actually hated speaking to groups of people himself. "I can talk to two or three persons," he said, "but when there are more they radiate some unknown form of influence which paralyzes my vocal cords." He had no trouble communicating with people over the telegraph wires or in his newspaper articles. The telephone made it easy to speak to someone without seeing them and getting nervous.

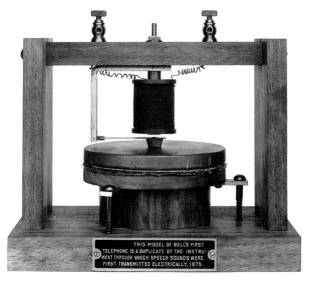

Library of Congress, LC-D420-2586

Alexander Graham Bell's telephone.

"AHOY!" **THE WORD "HELLO"** was first used in 1883, as a greeting when answering the telephone. A variant of earlier words like "hallo" and "halloo," which were shouts to attract attention, it was made up by the Edison crew working on the telephone. Alexander Graham Bell wanted people to answer the telephone with the greeting "Ahoy." The Edison greeting, "hello," became more popular. Imagine answering machines today saying, "Ahoy! We're not available to answer the phone right now, so at the beep, please leave a message."

The Phonograph

The phonograph, Edison's next important invention, promised to capture the human voice so it could be played over and over. The phonograph was a remarkable invention because it was the first time in history a person's voice could be recorded and saved. And, importantly for Edison, the volume could be regulated so everyone could hear the recording. The phonograph was his proudest invention and made life easier for Edison because it allowed him to avoid speaking in public. He could record his own speeches and have them played to groups. In 1908, Edison used the phonograph to deliver a speech to crowds at the Electrical Show in New York City and again the next year in Chicago.

Edison explained how the idea for the phonograph came to him: "I was experimenting on an automatic method of recording telegraph messages on a disk of paper laid on a revolving platen." He'd experimented with similar ideas back in his teen years, while trying to improve the telegraph. Now, he used electricity and magnets to press marks into the paper according to telegraph signals. It could be played back at a fast speed, and Edison realized he could design the machine so it made marks to match the sounds of a human voice. He continued experimenting and came up with a sketch of a metal cylinder with a spiral groove around it. As the cylinder turned with a handle at one end, a needle and diaphragm would move along the groove. A thin coating of tinfoil covered the cylinder so the needle could gently etch marks into the tinfoil in response to sound vibrations.

No one believed it would work—not even Thomas Edison. When ready to test it, his staff crowded around as Edison began turning the handle that moved the cylinder. He shouted, "Mary had a little lamb, its fleece was white as snow." He stopped turning, lifted the needle, and put a second needle and diaphragm back at the beginning position. This time, without saying a word, he turned the handle so the needle followed the engraved marks made by the first needle. The machine played back his words perfectly—to everyone's shock.

"I was never so taken aback in my life," Edison said. "I was always afraid of things that worked the first time."

The workshop crew immediately set to work improving and perfecting the phonograph, named after the Greek words for "sound" (*phono*) and "writing" (*graph*). When he was ready to introduce the phonograph to the world, Edison took it to New York, to the offices of *Scientific American*

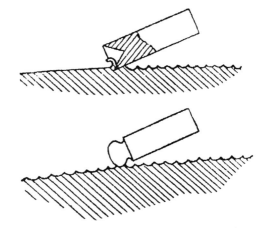

Edison: His Life and Inventions, Harper Brothers, 1910

These drawings show how the phonograph worked. The top image shows a recording needle cutting grooves into tinfoil to record sounds. (The foil was thicker than the type we use in the kitchen today.) The sounds passed from the microphone through a diaphragm that made the needle move in response to the sound vibrations. The bottom image shows a different type of needle that went over the grooves, causing the sound to play back.

magazine. A dozen people gathered around as he began cranking the handle and the machine asked about their health, asked how they liked the phonograph, claimed it was feeling very well, and said good night. The listeners were astounded.

Edison's staff began holding exhibits at the lab for crowds who rode out on special trains just to see the amazing machine. Not everyone believed the phonograph really worked. Some thought it was a trick or hoax of some kind. They searched the room for a trickster who might be making the sounds said to come from the machine. Edison had to show many doubters that it really did record the human voice and that it just wasn't a ventriloquist's trick.

Edison was always proud of his unique invention. He said, "I've made a good many machines, but this is my baby, and I expect it to grow up to be a big feller, and support me in my old age."

People had been quick to see the value in using telephones—they could talk to someone—but even though the phonograph was an incredible invention, what could it be used for? At first, no one thought much about using it to play music. The first phonographs didn't work fast enough to make music sound very real. Besides, Edison didn't think of the phonograph as a machine for entertainment—

he wanted to make useful things. Certainly, he always remembered the vote recorder no one wanted, and he was determined to make things people would use. He thought phonographs would be useful to record speeches, to record books for blind people to listen to, to record voices of family members so they could be remembered after they died, and for education. He thought teachers could record messages, facts, and lectures that students could play back so they could learn easily. He figured learning foreign languages would be easier with the phonograph, because people could hear the spoken words. He also hoped the phonograph could be connected to the telephone so voices from a distance could be recorded and saved.

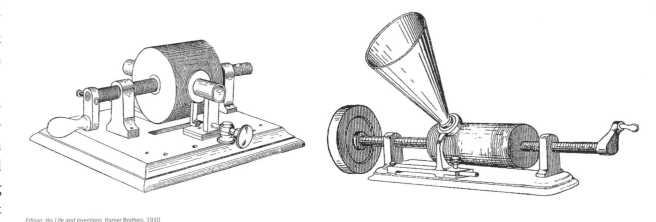

Edison: His Life and Inventions, Harper Brothers, 1910

Early phonographs. The handle turned the cylinder while a playing needle traveled over the tinfoil surface to make the sounds.

MAKE MUSIC WITH A NEEDLE

EDISON'S EARLY phonographs used a needle to gently etch marks onto a tinfoil cylinder. Later, the needle etched onto wax cylinders, then wax disks. The disk led to the development of plastic phonograph records. Today, most kids listen to music on CDs or downloaded to handheld devices, but your parents or older relatives probably remember record albums fondly. Do this simple project and see for yourself exactly how a needle can make music.

YOU'LL NEED

❋ Straight pin

❋ Disposable plastic cup

❋ Clay

❋ Turntable and old, unwanted record album (Check with older relatives. You can also find old turntables at thrift shops.)

❋ High-power magnifier (optional)

Push a pin through the bottom of a plastic cup from the inside. Press a small piece of clay inside the cup to hold the pin (needle) steady. Place an old record on the turntable and turn it on. Be sure the turntable's needle is not touching the record as it spins around. Keeping your hand still, hold the cup gently above the record so the straight pin drags lightly along a groove as the record spins.

What did you hear? How clear was the sound? How loud was it? Did the sound get louder, softer, or stay the same if you pushed harder on the needle? Why might you *not* want to push hard on the needle?

The groove on a record disk has thousands of tiny bumps and dips. Look at a record groove using a high-power magnifier. As a needle drags along this groove, it vibrates. The needle causes the cup to vibrate, and sound is produced. Early needles were made of metal or bamboo. Modern needles are made with diamonds (these diamonds are not as valuable as the ones used in jewelry and are much smaller).

Edison continued to demonstrate the phonograph to audiences who were amazed at the new technology. He took it to Washington, DC, where he gave a demonstration to members of Congress. It was late at night, but President Rutherford B. Hayes insisted he bring it to the White House for a demonstration. Mrs. Hayes was roused from bed in the middle of the night to come downstairs and listen to the marvel. Congress and the president were very impressed. The reaction to Edison's phonograph was entirely different from the poor reception he'd gotten in the same city when he introduced his vote-recording machine years earlier.

The phonograph was almost too easy for Edison to invent. He had discovered it almost accidentally, while working on improvements to the telephone and telegraph. Most of his work at that time was for large companies that wanted him to invent and manufacture things for them to distribute, and he didn't really know what to do with the phonograph. He decided to produce phonographs at his own workshop but needed to figure out how to sell them to the public.

Edison began manufacturing and selling phonographs to agents who went around the country setting up shows for the public. Across the country, fairgrounds and halls filled with audiences who paid to hear what

Professional musicians saw the phonograph as a threat because it made music available to people without attending a concert—or paying the musicians. They called phonograph music "canned music," maybe because the recording cylinder looked like a tin can. The musicians' protests didn't last long, however, because they soon realized they could be paid for their recorded music each time a recording was sold, through the copyright system of royalties.

the showman had recorded. Voices, music, foreign languages—even the sounds of cattle and dogs—held them spellbound.

Edison kept improving the phonograph bit by bit over the years as he worked on other projects. He had set it aside for a while when a toy manufacturer asked him to create a small version of the phonograph that could be put inside a doll body. Edison was interested in the project and worked out a small phonograph to create "talking dolls." A recorded cylinder attached to a spring was inserted in the doll's body and attached to a crank on the doll's back. When a child turned the crank and wound it up, the doll would recite recorded nursery rhymes.

Edison had big plans for the talking doll. He set out to make 500 talking dolls a day in the factory. Dozens of young women sat in booths, repeating nursery rhymes in girlish voices onto the recording cylinders. They recorded "Mary Had a Little Lamb," "Jack and Jill," "Little Bo Peep," and other rhymes that lasted six seconds. The dolls had bodies of tin with arms, legs, and head of painted porcelain. With a human hair wig and dainty clothing, the dolls looked very elegant. But, sadly, the little phonograph inside the doll

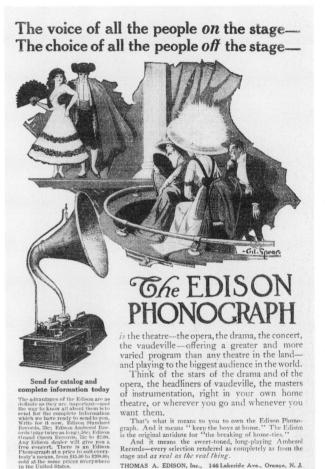

This advertisement shows how different improved phonographs looked by 1911.

Only a few of Edison's talking dolls exist today. This one is in the Edison Phonograph Museum in Quebec, Canada.

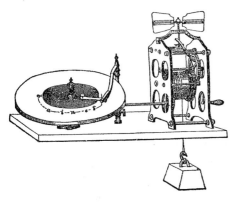

This drawing of Bain's telegraph appeared in *Parker's Philosophy*.

was too delicate to last long. Many fell apart during shipping and never spoke a word. The young owners were disappointed, and so was Thomas Edison. He shut the talking doll factory down.

Edison continued with his improvements to the phonograph. He decided to replace the tinfoil covering on the cylinder with a wax coating. It made the recordings more precise and the sounds clearer. Even better, the wax cylinder could be reproduced with a mold and copies could be made. He also figured out how to make a flat disk or plate to record on, instead of the cylinder. The disk worked so well it led to the development of phonograph records that could be cheaply molded from plastic (polyvinyl chloride). Plastic disk records were popular until CDs replaced them in the 1990s.

Edison's idea for disk phonograph records may have harked back to his favorite boyhood book, *Parker's Philosophy*. A drawing of Bain's telegraph had appeared in the book. It was a telegraph in which electric telegraphic pulses passed through a pen onto a paper disk that turned as the pen moved along a spiral path. The pen etched marks with a saltwater solution that stained the paper disk. Perhaps the concept stuck in Edison's mind.

To Your Health! Edison's Polyform Tonic

Thomas Edison was always concerned about health, just as most people were in those days because there were few medicines that actually worked. Protecting health was very important because although people understood that germs caused disease, most diseases had no cure, so prevention was essential. Antibiotics hadn't been invented yet (that would happen during World War II), so people tried to create remedies made from herbs, minerals, and other things that might help keep them healthy. Because Edison experimented with chemicals so much, it is no surprise he came up with a tonic, too. He named it Polyform and began selling it in 1878.

Polyform was made from cloves, peppermint, ether, chloroform, alcohol, and morphine. He sold the name and formula for $3,000, and the buyer continued selling the product for years. It was a powerful mixture, said to cure pains, but it's a wonder it didn't kill the patient! Ads claimed it helped to dull the pain of rheumatism, toothache, and headache. At that time, drugs and tonics weren't regulated by law. Anyone could concoct a remedy and market it until passage of the Pure Food and Drugs Act of 1907.

Inspiration from the West

In the summer of 1878, a group of scientists planned a train trip to Wyoming Territory to view a total eclipse of the sun. Edison went along, bringing a device he called the tasimeter, which he created to measure the heat from the sun. He set up his equipment beside a chicken house and said the chickens all went inside to roost during the afternoon eclipse, thinking it was nighttime as the moon moved to shut out the sun.

The tasimeter didn't work properly—the sun's heat was too much for it—but Edison made the most of his vacation out West. He had worked very hard to create the phonograph, and its success had nearly overwhelmed him with attention and visitors to his lab and home. Though still a young man at 31, he admitted he needed to get away for his health. It was a trip that stretched his thinking about many ideas. He traveled on to California by train, seated on a cushion on the cowcatcher at the front of the locomotive,

with a view of everything ahead on the tracks. He had a great time visiting gold mines, hunting, and visiting Yosemite State Park in California. It became a national park in 1890, and one of the high mountain lakes is named Thomas A. Edison Lake. Two months later, after touring the Sierra Nevada mountains and other sites, he was back in his New Jersey laboratory.

For the past several years, he had been dabbling in electricity projects, and now his head was full of new ideas. He'd seen miners working hard, with rivers flowing nearby—why couldn't electricity from the running water power their machinery, he wondered. On the windy northern plains, he saw farmers with no access to railroads to move their crops—wouldn't a wind-powered electric short-line railroad solve their problems? He spent years thinking about how electricity could be used to make life easier.

"Just at that time I wanted to take up something new," Edison said. He was about to begin his most important work: the electric light.

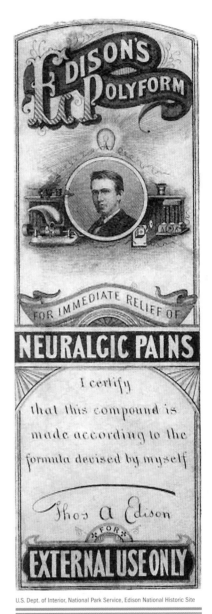

Advertisement for Edison's Polyform tonic.

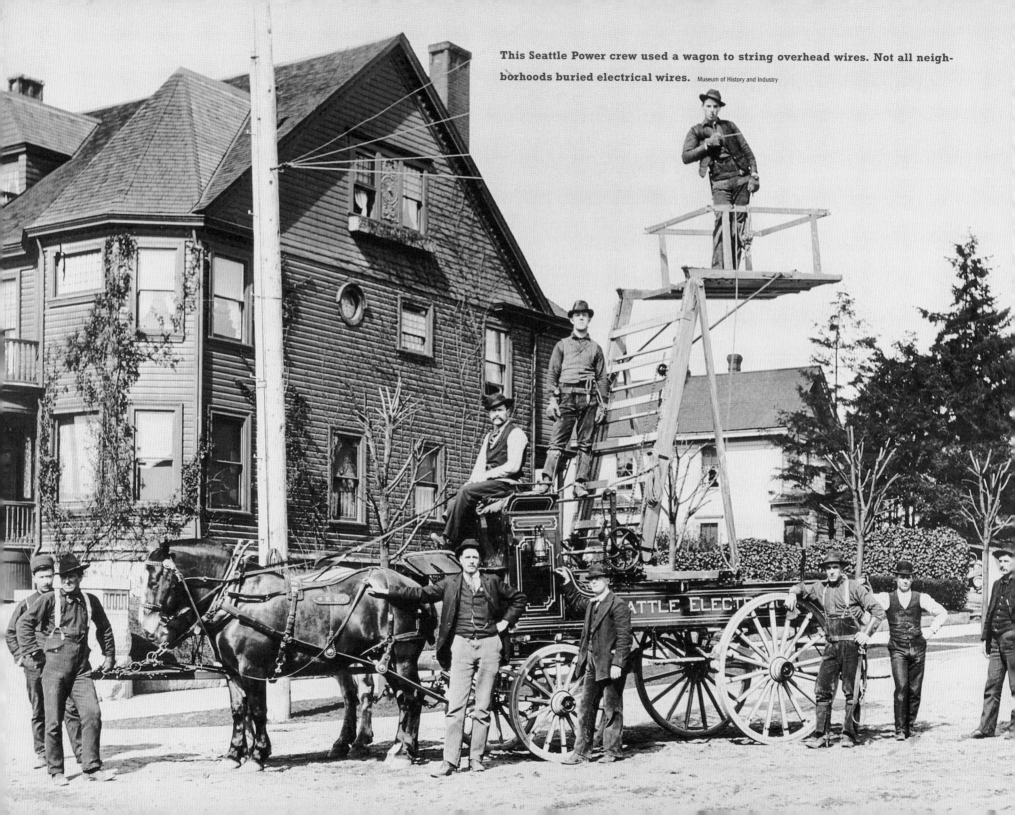

This Seattle Power crew used a wagon to string overhead wires. Not all neighborhoods buried electrical wires. Museum of History and Industry

Lights On!

Developing an Electric Lighting System

SEVERAL PEOPLE worked on inventing an electric light. An English scientist, Humphrey Davy, took the first step almost 100 years before Edison, when he invented the arc light. It was made of two sticks of charcoal that lit a flame between them when wires to a battery connected them. The arc light worked but had disadvantages. It was too bright for indoor use. (Today it's used for searchlights that sweep across the sky, and by welders who must wear eye protection because of the brilliance.) Plus, only one light could work at a time. It was fine for a coastal lighthouse or a streetlight here and there, but not something a household or business could use.

Victorian Houseware, Hardware, and Kitchenware, Dover Publishing, 1992

Before electric lights, people used candles, lanterns, and oil or alcohol lamps.

Streetlights were lit with gas made from coal vapors or by arc lights. Indoors, people lit lamps filled with whale oil, alcohol, or kerosene. Even tallow candles remained in use. But tallow candles, made from animal fat, were expensive and didn't put out much light—and they were fire hazards, too. Using whale oil to light lamps had nearly wiped out the whale population. Kerosene or coal gas was dangerous because lamps sometimes blew up, burning anyone near them. And their greasy soot was a nuisance, making walls dirty and people cough. Everyone wanted a light that was cleaner, safer, and brighter.

During the 1800s dozens of inventors tried to come up with a better lighting idea. Several men had created electric lights that burned a filament (a thin piece of material) inside a glass globe. As the filament burned, it created a bright light. But none lasted more than a few hours. As soon as the filament had burned up, the light went out. Besides, they remained useless because no one could figure out how to keep rows of lights from going out if one light failed. Finding a filament that burned a long time, and figuring out how to control the electric current through several bulbs at once, challenged inventors.

Edison had been working on the telephone when he began work on the light bulb. He had created the carbon transmitter that made Alexander Graham Bell's telephone work better, so he tried carbon for several other projects that year. Carbon was on his mind. When he needed to find a filament for his light bulb design, he again turned to carbon.

He used a strip of paper coated with carbon attached by wires to a battery, then put it inside a glass globe from which all the air was pumped out, creating a vacuum. The light burned inside the globe for 10 to 15 minutes. Other light bulb inventors had gotten bulbs to burn, but only for short times. The key was burning the filament inside a vacuum, with very little oxygen present. That's what made Edison's light bulb superior to the ones others had tried. With the vacuum bulb he was a step ahead, but he knew he needed a better filament to make the bulb burn long enough to be useful. The search was on to find a material for filament that would burn longer.

Lab experiments with more than 6,000 items failed. Finally, Edison discovered that tiny shreds of bamboo, coated with carbon, worked well. Bamboo plants grow easily in warm climates, but the kind that worked best for Edison was not easy to find. It grew only in Japan, or so people said. He sent a man to Japan to buy supplies of it. (Bamboo filaments lit light bulbs for almost 10 years before a longer-burning carbon filament was created from cellulose. Today, metal filaments are

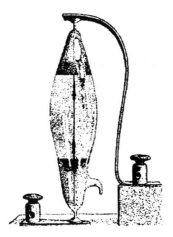

A Short History of Technology, Dover Publications, 1993

This drawing shows inventor Joseph Swan's light bulb. Thomas Edison was one of several people working on creating a working light bulb at the same time.

A Short History of Technology, Dover Publications, 1993

This shows what Edison's early light bulbs looked like. How do they compare to those we use today? Not much difference. Edison created a good design that hasn't changed very much.

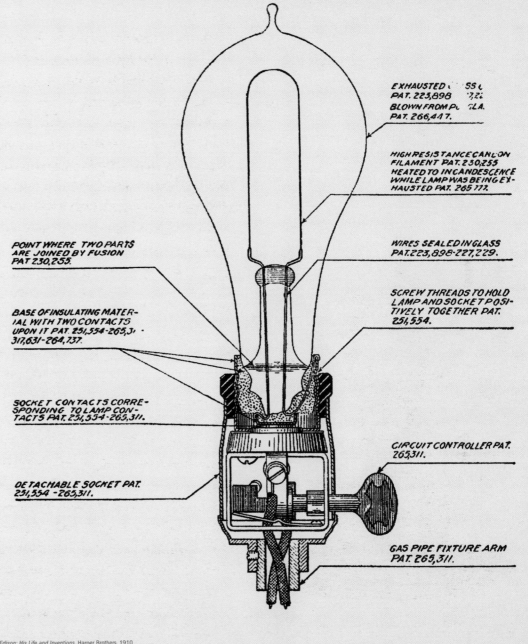

EXHAUSTED GLASS PAT. 223,898 BLOWN FROM P. GLA. PAT. 266,447.

HIGH RESISTANCE CARBON FILAMENT PAT. 230,255 HEATED TO INCANDESCENCE WHILE LAMP WAS BEING EXHAUSTED PAT. 265,777.

WIRES SEALED IN GLASS PAT. 223,898 - 227,229.

SCREW THREADS TO HOLD LAMP AND SOCKET POSITIVELY TOGETHER PAT. 251,554.

POINT WHERE TWO PARTS ARE JOINED BY FUSION PAT. 230,255.

BASE OF INSULATING MATERIAL WITH TWO CONTACTS UPON IT PAT. 251,554 - 265,31. - 317,631 - 264,737.

SOCKET CONTACTS CORRESPONDING TO LAMP CONTACTS PAT. 251,554 - 265,311.

DETACHABLE SOCKET PAT. 251,554 - 265,311.

CIRCUIT CONTROLLER PAT. 265,311.

GAS PIPE FIXTURE ARM PAT. 265,311.

Edison: His Life and Inventions, Harper Brothers, 1910

Diagram of Edison's light bulb showing the parts he invented and patented.

used in light bulbs.) Next Edison added another twist to his light bulb, creating the screw-in base that made it easy to change light bulbs.

Edison's light bulb, called an incandescent light, was a hit. It was superior to anything else on the market. But he knew it was only part of the process. He needed to create an entire system of electricity before people could use light bulbs inside their homes.

SCOURING THE GLOBE

EDISON HAD TRIED CARBON for light bulb filament because it was handy, and he'd been using it in other experiments and in the telephone. When he wanted to perfect the light bulb, however, he knew he needed special materials because none of the things he had available in the workshop supply stores worked. He knew he wanted a natural fiber, but from which plant? He sent people all over the world to find out.

Sending explorers around the globe to bring back unusual plants was nothing new. Kings, governments, and sea captains had been doing so since before Columbus discovered the New World. Columbus took plant specimens such as corn, potatoes, and tomatoes back to Europe. Europeans had never seen those plants before but quickly added them to their diet.

In 1880, Edison sent a man to China and Japan to find the perfect type of bamboo plant to make filaments for light bulbs. The Japanese bamboo was the best he could find, but Edison thought there might be an even better type of bamboo, and he sent explorers to search for it. At the same time he sent another plant explorer up the Amazon River of Brazil, where he spent a year looking for a special kind of palm tree. A school principal spent a year searching Southeast Asia for plants Edison needed. Expeditions went to Cuba and Jamaica, too. Edison sent three men to search the Florida swamps for five months, and they shipped 500 boxes of plant samples back to New Jersey.

Edison's Electric System

Edison worked hard to make a light bulb that worked, but he wanted more than that. He wanted to create a system for electric lighting. One light here and there would not help enough and would be just an amusement or novelty. He needed to figure out how to send electricity along wires so that many, many lights could be operated at once. A system like that would make electric lights practical and useful.

He perfected the idea of several bulbs connected to one wire when he figured out how to regulate the current of electricity through the line. He created a piece of equipment called a "dynamo" to regulate the electric current flowing out of the heat source. A fuel like coal could be burned in a generator that fed electricity to the dynamo. The dynamo would adjust the heat energy, sending out a constant stream of electric current. Edison figured out the correct amount of electricity that should flow through the wires: 110 volts, which is the same level of electric current we use in homes today.

Edison's crew installed the first working incandescent lights in the laboratory at Menlo Park as well as inside Edison's home and in the boardinghouse down the street where several employees lived. Some lights were hung on poles in the streets for outdoor lighting. All were connected with wires to the main generator, which was located in the basement of the laboratory. Edison felt it was important that people see for themselves where the wires connected to the generator and then traveled to the light bulbs, because otherwise they might suspect a hoax. No one would accuse him of playing tricks when they saw the electric wires running directly to the light bulbs.

Local residents began coming to the laboratory at night to look at the amazing phenomenon. Edison realized it was time to alert the public, so he invited newspaper reporters to come see the new invention. A reporter from the *New York Herald,* who had also been on the trip out west, visited Menlo Park and wrote a glowing story about the new lights a few days before Christmas, 1879. It covered an entire page of the newspaper. The public rushed out to see for themselves and Edison was swamped with visitors. He opened the laboratory to the public after Christmas, and the Pennsylvania Railroad ran special trains carrying visitors. It was overwhelming. With only 20 or 30 employees, the Edison staff was unable to handle the huge crowds of children, farmers, sightseers, investors, inventors, bankers, and reporters.

Visitors ignored warnings and touched everything in sight. Many began experimenting at the laboratory workbenches, digging into supplies and equipment, and breaking things. Within days, 14 lamps were stolen and Edison was forced to shut down the tours. Only visitors with special passes would be admitted in the future.

A Short History of Technology, Dover Publications, 1993

The dynamo room at Edison's lab.

Lineman working on a pole. Telephone, telegraph, and electric wires were sometimes hung on the same pole.

In the 1880s, city streets were filled with an overhead web of tangled wires. Wires for telephones, telegraphs, burglar alarms, fire alarms, and stock market tickers were tacked to poles and rooftops. Electrical wires that powered arc lights were tacked on poles, too. But wires carrying electrical current for arc lights were dangerous, and many accidents and deaths resulted. Touching the "hot" wire jolted and burned unfortunate people, especially line workmen. One arc light lineman's body slowly roasted on a pole as a crowd watched in horror. Electric current is a powerful and dangerous force. How to control it and make it safe and useful was the challenge.

Burying the dangerous wires seems sensible now, but Edison was the first to put electrical wires underground. He was inspired to think that way because he thought of electricity as something that moved along a pipeline; sort of the way gas or water did in underground pipes. He covered the wires with insulating material and put them inside iron pipes. Once buried, they were safe and effective.

After Edison's first underground wiring system was in place in New York City, however, an emergency occurred. A repairman was summoned to find a leak in the underground wiring system because it had electrified a section of a street. A group of kids had spotted it and were directing horse-drawn carts to the section. When a horse's hooves touched the charged soil, it was shocked, reared up, and tried to run off. A crowd gathered to watch the excitement until the repairman shut the electric current off.

Electric lighting was cleaner and safer than anything else anyone had ever used, but not everyone was thrilled with Edison's new electric lighting system. Companies that sold gas for gaslights were upset because incandescent lights would put them out of business. Arc lighting companies resisted Edison's incandescent lights, too, because they lost business to the new product. Arc lights were only useful outdoors because they were very bright and often let off sparks. Arc light companies raced to get towns to build their system first because once towns had installed one system they didn't want to spend the money to build a different system. At times, it was a race to see which company could light a town's streets first, an arc or incandescent light company.

Competitors resisted Edison's light system, but people wanted his lights. People loved electric lights because they had no bad odor, didn't smoke, and didn't explode, like gas or kerosene lamps. The Edison system

BUILD AN ELECTRICAL CIRCUIT TO TEST MATERIALS:
INSULATOR OR CONDUCTOR?

EDISON'S ELECTRICAL systems relied on many different types of materials. Sometimes materials were needed to conduct an electrical current; other times materials were needed to serve as insulators. An electric current moves easily through a conductor. Insulators make it difficult or impossible for electric current to flow through them. Workers in Edison's labs tested thousands of different materials. You can build an electrical circuit to test whether materials are electrical conductors or insulators.

Adult supervision required

YOU'LL NEED
* Battery connector (available at hardware stores and Radio Shack)
* 9-volt alkaline battery
* Tiny light bulb and socket (available at hobby stores and Radio Shack)
* Assortment of materials to test, such as cotton ball, aluminum foil, eraser, coins, paper, rock, drinking glass, wooden spoon, plastic cup, or other household items

Snap the battery connector onto the battery. Connect one of the wires from the light bulb socket to one of the wires from the battery connector by twisting the ends of the wires together. Holding on to the plastic covering of the wires, pick up the other wires running from the battery connector and the light socket and touch the ends to the item you are testing for conductivity. Do not let the wires touch each other.

As you test the materials, watch the bulb. Does it light up? If it does, the material is a conductor. If it doesn't, the object is an insulator. When an electrical charge moves from the atoms in one material to those in another material, it is called electrical conduction. Test some metal items, as well as wood, plastic, glass, and rubber. Which are good insulators? Which are conductors? Insulators are used to protect against electrical shock. Not all conductors act the same; some carry electrical current better than others. The best conductor is gold, but imagine the cost if electrical wires were made of gold! Copper, a less expensive metal, works well as a conductor material in electrical wiring.

"Resistance" is the way a material slows down or refuses to allow electrical current to pass through it. The higher a material's resistance to electricity, the harder it is for electricity to flow through it. Good conductors have a low resistance; good insulators have a high resistance. Resistance is measured in "ohms." A wire with 10 ohms resistance is 10 times better as a conductor than a wire with 100 ohms resistance.

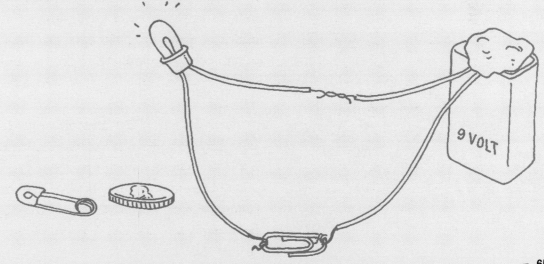

expanded quickly, with lighting exhibits and systems set up in Paris, London, Chile, Holland, Germany, and many small towns across America. Edison sold complete electrical lighting systems that included a large dynamo and 60 lamps, sockets, and wiring for $1,200.

Factories and department stores bought their own systems. Ships at sea adopted Edison's system, too. The Edison system was even used on a fishing ship, with lights suspended by cables 940 feet (286.5 m) into the water to lure fish for netting. Wealthy families like the Vanderbilts and Morgans bought systems to light their New York City mansions. Western ranches and Midwest farms bought their own Edison systems, too. Small communities purchased the systems and powered the generators with coal, wood, or steam. Between 1880 and 1882, the Edison Electric Lighting Company expanded by manufacturing and selling everything to make electric lighting possible: light bulbs, wiring, generators, batteries, and other necessary supplies.

A Short History of Technology, Dover Publications, 1993

← **The Pearl Street station in New York City used coal-fired generators to run the generating station that powered the neighborhood's electrical lights and motors.**

A New Industry

No one had worked out the ideas behind electricity before. Edison set up his own night classes to train workers to build and repair Edison lighting systems.

One problem was the high cost of wires to deliver electric current to homes. Copper was the best material for wire, and Edison developed a thin copper wire that worked while keeping costs down. As more people wanted electrical lighting, copper miners in the West began digging night and day to come up with enough copper to meet the growing demand. Huge mines in Montana, Nevada, Arizona, and Colorado resulted from the need for copper to wire the nation.

Ready-made parts and supplies didn't exist, either. Edison's workshops and factories built all the needed wire, switches, light bulbs, and so on, because they couldn't buy them anywhere. They succeeded, despite many other competitors working on the same ideas at the same time, because the Menlo Park workshop and lab facilities made it easy to develop ideas in a team approach. Teams could work on different components of the system, such as light bulbs, wiring, dynamos, and so on, all in the same research compound. At that time, no other inventor or company had created a large research center like Edison's.

But the employees, workshops, labs, and raw materials for experiments cost money. Edison needed funds, so he began selling shares in his electric company. As his costs grew, he sold off more and more, until he was no longer in control of the Edison Electric Light Company. Investors were excited about being part of the new electrical age, but they also expected to make money from Edison's inventions.

In the end, Edison didn't make much money from his electrical patents; in fact, he spent years in court defending his patent rights to the electric light, while others copied his ideas. Instead he made money from manufacturing the parts and equipment needed in the electrical industry.

Machinery and Mechanical Devices, Dover Publications, 1987

Electrical power was used to power belt-driven machines like these.

"WHAT WILL HE GROW TO?"

Punch magazine, 1881, reprinted in Edison: The Man Who Made the Future, G. P. Putnam's Sons, 1977

This 1881 cartoon showed that people wondered what would happen to Steam and Coal, now that electricity had arrived.

Edison Faces Competition

Things did not go smoothly for Edison as he developed electrical lighting systems. From the beginning, newspapers carried stories that criticized him, ridiculed the idea, and said he would never succeed. Scientists would not accept his ideas, claiming he was not educated but "only" an inventor. Once he began demonstrating his lighting systems, rivals visited the labs and workshops and stole his ideas. One company hired a spy to work undercover in the laboratory. At the same time, other inventors were working on making incandescent light bulbs, too. There was a rush to borrow ideas, then patent and sell them to investors. Because such work took a lot of money, investors bought stock in rival electrical lighting companies. And investments and ideas had to be protected, which meant going to court with lawsuits for patent protection. Edison spent a huge amount of money defending his patents for electrical inventions in court. Cases dragged on for years while competitors continued to copy each other's ideas.

Not only had Edison moved far ahead of competitors by creating the complete electrical supply system, from light bulb to dynamo to wiring, he had eliminated his greatest foe: the gaslight companies. They fought hard, sending agents into the Edison labs to destroy equipment, printing newspaper stories about how electricity would never work for lighting, and fighting Edison's system every step of the way. But the days of gaslight were over—the electrical light had taken its place. Edison's systems appeared everywhere, on steamships, in hotels and stores, and in complete neighborhoods. By the late 1880s, the Edison lighting system was a success, and the Menlo Park laboratory was growing too small for both research and manufacturing. In 1886, Edison expanded, building a factory in Schenectady, New York, and a larger laboratory facility in West Orange, New Jersey.

But just as his lighting system had successfully replaced gaslights, Edison faced another hurdle. A new competitor began challenging the direct current system Edison and other electrical companies had been installing. By that time, there were six other electric lighting companies in New York City alone. Even competitors had been using Edison's direct current system, in which electric current flowed from the generator to the user, then back to the generator. It had to be kept at a low voltage so it wouldn't burn out the light filaments. Now a new system was challenging Edison's—alternating current.

Nikola Tesla (see sidebar on page 70) was a brilliant young engineer who worked for a year at Edison's New Jersey laboratory. Tesla suggested his idea of alternating current to Edison. Alternating current (AC) used a much higher amount of electricity—a higher voltage—than direct current (DC), and then reduced the amount of voltage sent off to houses. The current didn't move in one continuous direction, rather it moved in one direction, built up, then reversed direction, and kept repeating the movement—but so quickly it didn't affect the flow of current.

Edison didn't like the idea of AC because it carried higher voltage, which could be very dangerous. He proudly pointed out that no part of his DC electrical generating system could give a person a serious shock. It was entirely safe. The fact that he had invented the DC generator, and others had invented and patented the AC generator, also meant he wouldn't make as much profit or control the entire electrical system if it became AC.

Edison reportedly joked that he would give Tesla $50,000 if he could improve a dynamo. Tesla took up the offer, improved the dynamo, and then was mad when Edison said he had only been joking—the amount was too huge to take seriously in those days. Tesla asked for a raise, from $18 to $25 a week, but the foreman told him they couldn't afford to raise his pay and that other workers could easily be hired to replace him at $18. Tesla quit and went to work for George Westinghouse (see sidebar on page 72), Edison's competitor.

George Westinghouse, another inventor and businessman, had watched what Edison was doing and learned that inventors in Europe had been working on a different system, the alternating current (AC) idea. He thought AC would be superior to Edison's direct current (DC) system because direct current couldn't be sent very far through wires. Like sending natural gas through pipelines, and telephone messages through wires, Westinghouse hoped to send electrical current much farther than Edison was. And, if he could figure out an AC system that worked, he could patent it and reap the profits.

Westinghouse bought some AC transformers built in Europe, set them up in a workshop, and eventually refined the design and created a practical AC power network. It was powered by a hydropower generator, using the energy coming from a waterfall. In 1886, he formed the Westinghouse Electric and Manufacturing Company and began installing 30 electrical systems to compete with the Edison Company's. He needed a meter to measure the electrical current and an electric motor, powered by AC.

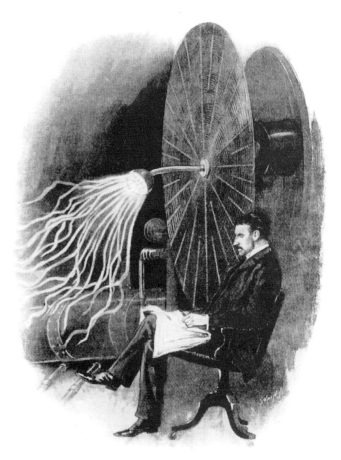

Pearson's Magazine, May 1899

This drawing shows Tesla reading comfortably while electrical current snaps and whirls around him. It was a publicity stunt, like the electrical shows he performed for audiences. The coil in the background was his invention that made wireless telegraphy possible.

NIKOLA TESLA

(1856–1943)

NIKOLA TESLA was an inventor who discovered the rotating magnetic field, the basis of most alternating current (AC) machinery. The Tesla coil, which he invented, is widely used today in radio and television sets and other electronic equipment.

Of Serbian descent, Tesla was born in Croatia. He was trained as an engineer at colleges and universities in Austria and Czechoslovakia. In 1882 Tesla went to work in Paris for the Continental Edison Company and during his spare time built the first induction motor. He moved to the United States where he continued to work for Edison's companies.

In May 1885, George Westinghouse bought the patent rights to Tesla's system of AC dynamos, transformers, and motors. With the Westinghouse money, Tesla started his own laboratory. He experimented with many of the same technologies Edison's teams worked on: x-rays, various types of lighting, and wireless transmission of electrical energy. In response to Edison's publicity efforts warning about the dangers of high AC voltage, Tesla gave exhibitions in his laboratory in which he lighted lamps without wires by letting electricity flow through his body. He presented popular programs using electricity in thrilling ways. In 1898 Tesla announced his invention of a boat guided by remote control, then proved his claims for it before a crowd in Madison Square Garden.

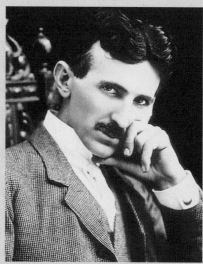

The Tesla Society

He went to Colorado where he made what he regarded as his most important discovery—terrestrial stationary waves. He proved that the earth could be used as a conductor and would be as responsive as a tuning fork to electrical vibrations of a certain frequency. He also lighted 200 lamps without wires from a distance of 25 miles (40 km) and created man-made lightning, producing flashes measuring 135 feet (41 m) long. At one time he was certain he had received signals from another planet in his Colorado laboratory, which made many experts ridicule him.

In 1900, Tesla began construction of a wireless broadcasting tower on Long Island, with $150,000 from financier J. Pierpont Morgan. He planned to provide worldwide communication, sending pictures, messages, weather warnings, and stock reports through the airwaves. The project was abandoned when Morgan quit funding it and was Tesla's greatest defeat.

Tesla enjoyed demonstrating electricity to crowds and discussing his projects with reporters, but in his personal life he was very much a loner. He had few friends (but one was writer Mark Twain). He had a phobia about germs and insisted on living in a peculiar manner, always counting his steps and insisting things always be done in threes. He refused to shake hands or touch other people. He made many wild claims and predictions but could also prove his theories correct.

When Nikola Tesla quit working for Edison, Westinghouse quickly contacted Tesla and bought the patent rights to Tesla's AC motor design. Westinghouse hired him as a consultant for a year and quickly put the improved idea to work, perfecting the AC system.

Tesla's AC did work differently and was an improvement over Edison's DC. It made sending electricity over wires for long distances possible. Transformers were designed so that the current was stepped up to travel over the power lines and then stepped down before it entered homes. It was efficient and successful. It also directly competed with Edison's DC systems. Because it ran from one central power generating system, it could be located on a dam in a river or at a coal plant out of town—and the voltage sent over wires to the transformers miles away. It made electricity cheaper and easier to deliver to large numbers of customers.

Edison thought it wouldn't work. He believed that building power plants in remote areas and sending current a long distance wasn't practical. Westinghouse began setting up his systems in the South and West, hoping to get a foothold in the prize of markets: New York City. Edison had already installed so many of his direct current systems in New York City that it seemed unlikely Westinghouse would succeed there. No one wanted to remove a working system to install another. And, before Westinghouse bought Tesla's AC motor design, AC could only operate lights, while Edison's DC was operating electrical motors, so important to industry and manufacturing.

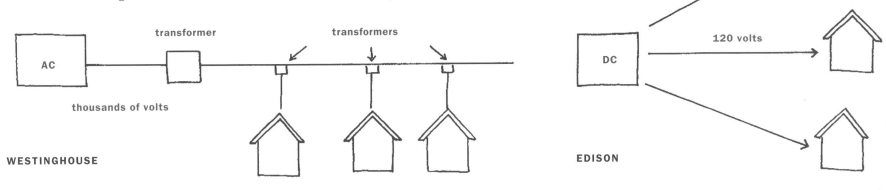

This drawing shows the difference between alternating current (AC), which serves several houses from one main line, and direct current (DC), which runs from a power source to a single station.

GEORGE WESTINGHOUSE

(1846–1914)

GEORGE WESTINGHOUSE was born in Central Bridge, New York, in 1846. His father owned a factory, which allowed young George to grow up around machines and business. When the Civil War started, 15-year-old George and his two older brothers joined the Union army. The brothers were killed, but George returned to Schenectady after the war and enrolled in college, studying engineering and railroads.

Westinghouse turned his attention to making railroads safer, inventing a device to move derailed train cars back onto the track, and improving the brakes on trains, something vital for safety. At the time, railcars had to be stopped by a brakeman, who ran along the tops of the cars, pulling up on brake levers to stop the turning wheels below. Many brakemen were killed in accidents and trains were difficult to stop. George Westinghouse created a braking system that worked better, using compressed air to slow the turning wheels.

In 1868, Westinghouse opened his own air-brake factory and became wealthy due to sales of his improved train brakes. He then invented an automatic signal and switching system and improved the way railcars were coupled together.

As his fortunes increased, he moved into other fields, such as improving drilling and piping systems for natural gas. After telephones were in use, Westinghouse designed a switchboard system to route telephone calls through a central exchange. His interest in creating systems to distribute natural gas and telephone calls turned his attention to the newly established electrical systems Thomas Edison and other electrical inventors were setting up.

Westinghouse was a successful businessman and inventor until the financial panic of 1907 led to his resignation.

Library of Congress, LC-US262-93492

The War of the Currents

After Nikola Tesla invented a motor that could operate on AC, the two systems began a real battle. George Westinghouse and Thomas Edison began fighting for the market in what has been called the "War of the Currents." As Westinghouse began making more sales, Edison fought back by pointing out that AC was dangerous. It was, but the transformers made it safe. Still, people weren't entirely comfortable with the idea of electricity anyway. The gaslight industry had tried to scare people away from using electric lights by telling them it was harmful. Now they wondered if it really was dangerous. Accidental deaths and electrical fires made people more wary. Edison began telling newspaper reporters that AC was dangerous, saying the high voltage power lines were potential killers. Edison and other direct current companies tried to get laws passed making electrical circuits over 800 volts illegal. That failed. Then one of Edison's employees came up with what seemed like a great idea for stopping George Westinghouse and the AC system.

Even though Edison and Westinghouse were the major competitors, there were several other electrical lighting companies in New York City. Some still sold arc lights for outdoor use; others sold systems using light bulbs and components purchased from Edison's factories. Because the field was still new, inventors were busy trying to perfect their own patents and versions of electrical lighting. Edison's systems ran on DC, and so did other electrical companies', such as the arc light systems. Westinghouse and AC was a threat to all of them.

H. P. Brown was an arc light inventor who took up the fight against AC. He wrote letters to newspapers saying the high voltage wires were dangerous because Westinghouse's AC wires carried a lot more electrical charge than the DC lines. High voltage wires strung over the streets of New York were already a hazard—falling wires killed dozens of people and horses each year in the city.

Edison hired Brown to help fight Westinghouse. Brown was given lab space in Edison's compound and told to prove AC was dangerous. Brown turned to the local children, paying them 25 cents for every stray cat or dog they brought to him. He experimented on shocking the animals, studying how much voltage it took to kill them. After destroying 50 animals in the experiments, Brown began giving public demonstrations, showing people how quickly electric current—which he

always said was AC and not DC—could kill. Brown even challenged George Westinghouse to a sort of a duel, asking Westinghouse to take AC electric current through his own body, beginning with 100 volts and increasing. Brown said he would take a continuous current of DC. Brown suggested each man would continue receiving the voltage until

Florida State Archives

Even if people adopted Westinghouse's AC systems, they still bought Edison's light bulbs. This store window display shows the many types to choose from.

one cried out and admitted he was wrong. Westinghouse ignored the challenge.

Brown decided to make electrical current even more frightening by demonstrating how it could kill people, not just animals. He offered to create an electrically wired chair that would execute convicts in the New York prison system. Officials wanted to find a better way to execute convicts because the current method of hanging was not working very well. In some cases the prisoners suffered unnecessarily. Brown saw this as an opportunity to beat Westinghouse's AC.

Edison himself told the New York governor that electrical execution would work quickly, without causing suffering to the prisoner. He pointed out that the AC machines made by George Westinghouse would be perfect for the task. "The passage of the current from these machines through the human body, even by the slightest contacts," Edison said, "produces instantaneous death."

So the New York Medical and Legal Society began studying how to execute criminals with electricity. They hired Brown, who began by demonstrating how electrical current could kill calves and horses. After a few tests, they all agreed the technique would work on humans. But to be certain, they needed to use an AC machine, and the only place to get one was from the Westinghouse Company. George Westinghouse saw what was happening and refused to sell his generators to his opponents, but Brown was able to secretly buy some AC machines.

In January 1889, murderer William Kemmler was set for execution by electricity. His lawyers argued that killing him by electricity was cruel and inhumane punishment, but the judge refused to change the plans. The execution went forward. Kemmler was strapped to a special chair, his hands strapped in buckets of salt water, and a charge of 1,600 volts was sent by wire to the buckets for 50 seconds. Yet he failed to die. Kemmler gasped and coughed. A second jolt was then passed through electrodes taped to his head and legs, killing him. It was an awful sight, but execution by electricity had its start. After that, the buckets of salt water were no longer used, and electricity was sent directly to the prisoner's body through electrodes.

Brown and Edison thought they could use the entire ugly episode to make people suspicious of Westinghouse's AC systems. They suggested that the new execution system be called "Westinghouse." If people referred to the punishment as "being Westinghoused," or "condemned to the Westinghouse," people would always think of the deadly potential of AC. But the word didn't catch on; people began using the term "electrocution" instead.

The War of the Currents continued, but it wasn't long before Westinghouse was the winner. He got the contract to light up the Chicago World's Fair in 1893, where he showed off his system. Then he got a contract to build a water power plant at Niagara Falls, New York, which sent thousands of volts over power lines 25 miles (40 km) away. His AC system became widely accepted and is the common type we have today.

Was Edison right or wrong? He was correct that AC current is very dangerous, especially when overhead power lines fall to the ground. *Never* touch one or go near one. Even when the voltage is lower (110) voltage inside homes, it can still be a killer. *Never* stick a finger or object into an electric socket or tamper with an electric cord that is plugged in—you'll receive a jolt of current that can be deadly. Worn, frayed, or damaged electrical cords can also be dangerous; the bare wires can come in contact with people or pets, causing electrical shock or start a fire.

Electric-Powered Trains

Thomas Edison's electric motor, running on DC, was important to his lighting systems, but it also laid the groundwork for future electric-powered train systems.

When Edison was on his trip to measure the solar eclipse in Wyoming Territory, he had decided that electric-powered trains might be very useful for remote locations. As he traveled across the northern Great Plains, he saw how difficult it was for western farmers to get their crops to market. There were few wagon roads, and railroads were expensive to build. At that time, he thought electric trains—smaller in size than coal-powered locomotives—might be a cheaper and easier means of getting farmers' grain from the farm to the market.

In 1880, while working on incandescent lighting, Edison began designing and building an electric train and rail system on his laboratory grounds. It wasn't an entirely new idea. Back in the 1830s, a blacksmith in Vermont—Thomas Davenport—was actually the first person to patent an electric train motor. He built a small model train with cars that ran around a track. He used batteries to power the motor and exhibited it in several cities. Next, an inventor in Scotland built a larger electric train that pulled cars built to hold two people—it was the first electric passenger train. It went four miles (6.4 km) per hour, not much faster than walking.

Other inventors worked on electric trains, too, and all continued to use battery power. These locomotives carried the batteries along with them, making the trains very heavy and requiring recharging of the batteries during a trip.

Edison moved in a different direction. He was developing an electric power system based on a fuel burning source (a generator) and a dynamo that converted the power into electric current. It was the basis for his electricity system for street and home lighting. When he turned to the electric train he decided to use the same system. He used the generator and dynamo to send current to operate the train engine, but he sent the current in wires that electrified the track, not the locomotive.

After a few years of tinkering and perfecting, Edison's full-size electric train was running full tilt on the track around the laboratory grounds. It went 40 miles (64 km) per hour on steep trestles and curves, scaring the daylights out of passengers. At one point, the track dropped 60 feet (18 m), about a six-story drop, making it very much like a roller coaster. After riding Edison's experimental train, one visitor said,

"I protested at the rate of speed over the sharp curves, designed to show the power of the engine, but Edison said they had done

Smithsonian Institution, 80-16628

Some of Edison's employees trying out the electric railroad.

it often. Finally, when the last trip was taken, I said I did not like it, but would go along. The train jumped the track on a short curve, throwing Kruesi, who was driving the engine, with his face down in the dirt and another man in a comical somersault through some underbrush. Edison was off in a minute, jumping and laughing, and declaring it was a 'daisy.'"

Edison's team worked hard on the train, hoping to sell it to some investors from Bogota, Colombia, who told Edison they wanted a train system to replace mule trails in the mountains of South America. But the South Americans disappeared after Edison got his system working, and he never heard from them again.

He turned his attention back to the Great Plains farmers and how electric trains might help them. Edison's friend Henry Villard owned the Northern Pacific Railroad and enthusiastically agreed with Edison. They both thought short runs could connect outlying Dakota wheat farms to the main Northern Pacific Railroad that ran across the northern Plains. As it was, farmers living too far from the rail line couldn't sell their crops, which made their land worthless.

Edison studied winds on the Great Plains and wondered if it was possible to power such trains with energy from windmills. Villard paid for Edison's experimental railroad at the lab, but was financially bankrupt by the mid-1880s, before he could build an electric railway on the Northern Plains.

After Edison's innovation—powering the engine with electric current through the tracks and not in a battery—electric trains and trolleys popped up across the country. Electric railways powered by underground generators and dynamos replaced horse-drawn trolleys in cities across the country and were the beginning of modern underground subway systems.

Edison's Industry and Celebrity Grow

The early 1880s were Edison's most productive years. While working on the bigger ideas, he kept workers busy figuring out how to create and make many other smaller machines and inventions. He simply couldn't work on all of his ideas at once, and he often had to put a promising project aside in favor of one he felt was more important. His working methods relied on both science and serendipity. "I never think about a thing any longer than I want to. If I lose my interest in it, I turn to something else," he said. "I always keep six or eight things going at once, and turn from one to the other as I feel like it. Very often I will work at a thing and get where I can't see anything more of it, and just put it aside and go at something else; and the first thing I know, the very idea I wanted will come to me. Then I drop the other and go back to it and work it out." In 1884, he abandoned the electric train, saying, "I could not go on with it. I had too many other things to attend to, especially in connection with electric lighting."

Thomas Edison became a celebrity after his work with the light bulb. His name and image were known worldwide while he was still in

Men: A Pictorial Archive from Nineteenth-Century Sources, Dover Publications, 1980

Men in a laboratory.

his 30s. Visitors were welcomed to his labs by invitation or for special reasons. Royalty, scientists, and foreign ambassadors often stopped by the labs. Sioux chief Sitting Bull, famous actresses, and the president of Mexico visited.

Edison was always especially friendly with visiting newspaper reporters. He liked giving them information and stories, and the publicity helped his businesses. He liked to tell reporters about great inventions that were almost completed. When the stories ran in the papers, his competitors usually figured he was much closer to a patent than he actually was. This strategy made the public aware of upcoming inventions, so they were eager to use them, while it discouraged his competition. Sometimes the press stories helped boost the stock market, improving Edison's financial situation. Edison had been a reporter himself, covering stories for his own newspaper, the *Weekly Herald,* back in his youth, so he liked working and joking with reporters. Sometimes Edison's casual jokes to reporters were printed up as fact, such as the time he joked that cucumbers could be a source of energy because they absorbed sunlight, like a storage battery.

As a wealthy inventor, Edison started a magazine called *Science.* He ran the magazine for a year and a half before selling it to Alexander Graham Bell's father-in-law. The magazine ran several stories about Edison's inventions and ideas. Today, it's still a leading scientific magazine.

The electric light project caused Edison to spend many 18-hour days in the workshops and labs, seldom seeing his wife, Mary, or three children. During the winter of 1883–84 he was sick with neuralgia, a condition causing painful spasms in the skin or nerves. He took Mary and their daughter Marion south, to northern Florida, where he spent the winter recovering. When refreshed, Mary and Marion returned to New Jersey, but Thomas Edison went to stay in New York, working on the electrical business. A few months later, Mary came down with typhoid fever, which was a serious infection caused by consuming contaminated food or drink. Antibiotics treat it today, but in 1884 there was no medication to save typhoid fever victims. Mary died at the Edison home, leaving grief-stricken Thomas and their three young children.

Thomas Edison seemed unable to deal with the loss of his beautiful young wife, spending all his time in the laboratory. Perhaps he regretted not spending more time with her at home, but there was nothing he could do to bring her back.

A man operating a lathe.

Vitascope Theater in New York City.

Library of Congress, LC-USZC4-1102

A New Life

Home, Family, and Moving Pictures

IN 1884, Thomas Edison was a 37-year-old widower with three young children. Dot (Marion) was 12, Dash (Tom) was nine, and Will was only seven years old. He had not given the children much of his time and attention over the years. Now they were his entire responsibility, yet he needed to be in the laboratory in order to keep the business running. Dot became a sort of "little mother," filling her own mother's shoes by accompanying her father to social events when she wasn't away at boarding school. The boys were sent to stay with their Aunt Alice, who also lived in Menlo Park.

The winter after Mary died, Thomas worried about his own health because after a Chicago business trip he had caught a bad cold that turned into pneumonia. After lying in bed for a week, he finally recovered. Pneumonia was often a deadly sickness in those days, with few treatments other than bed rest and drinking liquids. Thinking of the warm climate in Florida, Tom headed south as soon as he was able to travel. He and Dot went to an exhibition of his inventions in New Orleans and continued on to Florida. They ended up traveling on a rickety train and then a boat through the pine forests to Fort Myers, on the western coast of central Florida. It was as different from New Jersey as any place could be. He saw forests dripping Spanish moss along the Caloosahatchee River, isolated plantations of coconuts and date palms, breadfruit trees, and giant Japanese bamboo. The little village at Fort Myers was charming and its residents friendly to the famous northern inventor. Edison immediately purchased a 13-acre parcel of land and began planning to build a home there.

A home in Florida's Everglades promised excitement and pleasure for the Edison family. Thomas and the children could escape the harsh winter every year, something many people did for their health in those days. They could fish, which Edison loved to do, and even more important, he could search for exotic plants that might be useful. Bamboo filament had solved his problem with the light bulb; who could tell what other plants might have valuable industrial uses? Florida's woods were thick with exotic plants and animals, and the perfect place to search for other wonders.

Northerners who could afford it were beginning to establish winter homes in Florida. The famous writer Harriet Beecher Stowe, who wrote *Uncle Tom's Cabin*, a best-selling book about slavery before the Civil War, had already taken a winter home in Florida. She wrote about the joys of wintertime living in the warm climate and encouraged others to take up the winter home lifestyle, and many did.

Edison knew he would have a hard time pulling himself away from his work. But he said, "I looked forward to the time when I would be getting on in years and would want to come to Florida every winter, and I couldn't imagine a nicer place than Fort Myers. There were wild ducks by the acre, the river was full of fish, and it seemed to afford a perfect opportunity for rest and recreation." Edison, following his usual pattern, studied every book about Florida and then began building.

From the start, Edison planned to build two houses, one for his family and another for a longtime friend and employee, Ezra

Gilliland, and his family. Even though the houses would be fairly remote from most amenities, electricity for a workshop and laboratory would come from a large steam engine. Edison planned to bring along an electric lighting plant, too. He hired designers and had the two houses cut and put together in sections in Maine, then shipped to Florida where they were assembled. They were the first prefabricated homes in America. A ship full of supplies for building a laboratory was lost at sea in the Atlantic Ocean on its way to Fort Myers, so a second set of supplies had to be assembled and shipped. The Fort Myers project was no easy feat, but the challenge gave Edison something new and different to work on.

The village residents at Fort Myers were shocked that someone as famous and important as Edison had chosen to move into their neighborhood. They were elated and set out a warm welcome, with headlines in the little town's newspaper proclaiming, "Edison is Coming." One thing that may have clinched the decision to locate a winter home at Fort Myers was that the International Ocean Telegraph line ran undersea nearby, making it easy for Edison to stay in touch with his crew back in New Jersey through the telegraph. Messages could be passed back and forth almost instantly, allowing Edison to keep

SEMINOLE INDIANS

WHEN THE EDISONS moved to Fort Myers, Florida, there were some Native Americans, called Seminoles, living nearby. By that time the Seminole people in Florida had been driven into the remote swamps of the Everglades. During the 1800s they had been hunted down and murdered or removed to make the area peaceable for settlers. They fought back, attacking the intruders, so in 1853, Congress passed a law that said, "it shall be unlawful for any Indian or Indians to remain within the limits of the State, and that any Indian or Indians that may remain, or may be found within the limits of this State, shall be captured and sent west of the Mississippi." Some Seminoles managed to escape the persecution and hung on, living in the isolated swamps. Edison named his house "Seminole Lodge," because he liked and respected the Indians.

track of what was happening back at the main home and headquarters.

While Edison's Florida project was underway, he embarked on another important project: finding another wife. Thomas Edison was lonely and knew he couldn't raise his children alone. Women from all over the country were sending him cards and letters offering marriage proposals, which his secretary politely answered, but nobody interested him. The Gillilands understood the situation and began inviting Edison—and a few single women—to dinner and tea at their home. It was there, in the Gillilands' parlor, that Edison was enchanted by a beautiful young woman, Mina Miller. He began seeing her at parties and on picnics and carriage rides with the Gillilands.

Mina Miller was raised in a wealthy family in Akron, Ohio; her father had invented farm equipment and also managed the Chautauqua Association. Chautauquas were summer gatherings where people assembled to hear lectures and educational programs. Chautauquas were an important means of self-education, and the meetings grew in size and spread out to many communities across the nation. Mina's father had founded the series and stressed self-education. While he thought Thomas Edison was too old for his 18-year-old daughter, he admired that Edison was self-educated and had made his own success in life.

Thomas taught Mina the Morse code, and the two of them sent silent messages to one another by tapping their fingers on the other's hand. They "conversed" in this secret manner while on excursions, carriage rides, and steamboat trips surrounded by others. For Edison, it was especially fun, because he had so much difficulty following conversations due to his deafness.

In September 1885, the two agreed to marry. While Mina and her family planned the big wedding (after all, she was marrying the nation's most eligible bachelor, one both famous and rich), Thomas headed to Florida to oversee the home building project. Edison didn't want to start a new marriage in the old house at Menlo Park, where Mary's memories would haunt the family, so he decided to buy a new home in New Jersey, too. In December, just before their wedding, Thomas asked Mina whether she wanted a house in the city or the country. She chose the country, and the two found a grand mansion on a hill, a brick and wood castle called "Glenmont." The owner had gone broke and left the country, and the house was a bargain, selling for only a quarter what it had cost to build. Glenmont

U.S. Dept. of Interior, National Park Service, Edison National Historic Site

The Edisons' New Jersey home, Glenmont.

was a large, red, rambling mansion, with plenty of spacious rooms, outbuildings, greenhouses, and beautifully landscaped grounds. The new home was about a half mile (.8 km) from West Orange, where Edison began building a new laboratory complex.

In February 1886, all of Akron was excited about the big wedding. Guests were greeted at the train station by carriages, which whisked them to the Miller home where a red carpet was laid out over the ground to welcome them, and rooms were packed with fresh flowers and treats. An orchestra played as waiters brought in from Chicago passed among the guests. After the ceremony, Thomas and Mina left by train for Florida, to spend their honeymoon in the Fort Myers house.

The buildings in Fort Myers were far from complete, however, so the couple ended up staying with others. When they returned to Glenmont three weeks later, they started a new chapter in Thomas Edison's life. A lovely new wife, a mansion home, and success in business bolstered his confidence. The electric light project was over, other projects were crowding his schedule, and he felt ready to move ahead once again. Gazing out the window of Glenmont one day, he said to his secretary, "Do you see that valley?" The secretary agreed, "Yes, it's a beautiful valley."

"Well, I'm going to make it more beautiful," Edison told him. "I'm going to dot it with factories."

Life Expands

Thomas Edison set out to create a laboratory complex at West Orange, New Jersey, that was 10 times the size of his Menlo Park facility. It was the largest research laboratory in the world at that time and had workshops that could build practically anything Edison dreamed up. "We can build anything from a lady's watch to a locomotive," Thomas Edison bragged. Inventions could be completed in two or three days, with little expense, because he had nearly every kind of supply one might need.

The large central building was 250 feet (76 m) long and three stories high. Inside were machine shops, an engine room, glass-blowing rooms, chemical and photographic rooms, stockrooms, and, near the main entrance, a large office and library. The library had 10,000 books, and the storeroom was lined with glass cases filled with colored bottles of various chemicals and compounds. It was like a huge museum/library/workshop. Four more buildings sat beside the main building, creating a square enclosed by a high

Mina Edison playing piano for Madeleine and Charles Edison, two children from Thomas Edison's second marriage.

The Edison home in Fort Myers, Florida, which the Edisons called Seminole Lodge.

Orange was truly a serious community devoted to invention and production. Edison's staff grew to as many as 60 assistants, more than the dozen or so at Menlo Park. With more people working for him, he had to delegate work and couldn't watch over everyone's activities, as he once had done. His electrical company at Schenectady, New York, was run by trusted employees, who continued to sell Edison electrical systems and components across the country.

In 1888, Thomas and Mina Edison had their first child together, a daughter they named Madeleine. At that point, 3,000 employees worked on Edison's projects at various factories, labs, and offices. He spent more time with his family now than he did in years past, but Mina and the children still felt like they scarcely saw him. Mina didn't complain, but she admitted to others that it was difficult being married to a great man. Edison's children from his first marriage seldom stayed at Glenmont. It was very difficult for them to move from their old Menlo Park home, where their mother's memory remained. Marion spent her time at boarding school or touring Europe, while the boys stayed with their aunt in Menlo Park or their uncle Pitt Edison (Thomas's older brother) back in Michigan, when they weren't away at school.

picket fence with a security guard posted at the gate. Visitors were only welcome by invitation—no public tours, visiting tourists, thieves, or spies for competing businesses. By now, other inventors, such as Alexander Graham Bell and George Westinghouse, had copied the Menlo Park idea, creating invention factories of their own.

Menlo Park had been a lively place for seven years; now the larger facility at West

PARCHEESI

PARCHEESI IS an ancient game from India. It was played by people of all ages using game boards stitched from colored pieces of cloth. In the United States, cardboard game boards were first introduced just after the Civil War. In Edison's day, Parcheesi was a very popular game.

You can make a simple version to play with your friends.

YOU'LL NEED

* Game board
* Glue
* Cardboard
* Crayons or markers: red, blue, yellow, green
* Coin
* Pencil
* Colored paper: red, blue, yellow, green
* Scissors
* Pair of dice
* 2–4 players

TO MAKE THE BOARD AND PAWNS

Enlarge the game board shown here using a photocopy machine, or draw a larger version of your own. Glue it to the cardboard. Color in the four sections as shown: red, blue, yellow, and green. To make the pawns, trace the coin on colored paper to cut out 16 circles—four for each player: red, blue, yellow, and green.

GAME DIRECTIONS

Each player has four pawns of the same color (red, blue, yellow, or green). The goal is to get all four of your pawns to their Home before the other players do.

Starting with the red player, players take turns rolling two dice. You must roll a five on one of the dice to start your pawn on the board. If you roll a five on one die and something else on the other, your pawn can move as many points as shown on the other die. Move your pieces clockwise around the outer squares of the board, entering pawns where shown here, only with a roll of five. After rolling the dice once, it's the next player's turn. If you don't roll a five, you must wait till your next turn to try to roll a five and enter another pawn. Once on the board, move the pawns whatever number of spaces you roll on the dice.

You can split up the dice and move two pawns the number of spaces to match each die. You must move your pawns whenever possible.

Only one pawn can be in any space at one time. If a pawn is sitting in a space and the next player moves a pawn into that space, the first pawn is sent back to the beginning, to start all over again. The player who landed on the first pawn gets to move ahead 20 spaces.

The first player to get all four pawns into their Home area is the winner. Once a pawn is on the row heading Home, it can only enter Home when the dice reads the exact number of spaces needed to get there, plus one. Until the exact number is rolled, the pawn must wait to get Home.

There are lots of other strategic maneuvers, such as blockades, that made the game so appealing to Edison. More detailed rules can be found online at http://home.no.net/vkp3/parcheesi.html.

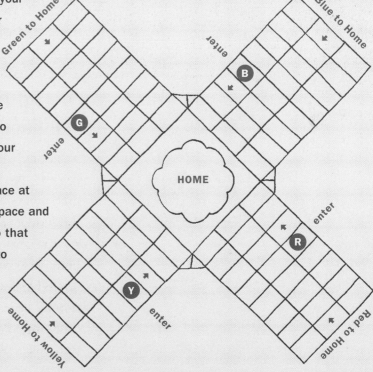

Edison spent most of his time working, inventing, or reading. He didn't spend much time on hobbies, sports, or amusements. When he bought Glenmont, however, it came with a pool table left by the previous owner. He got a book about billiards, taught himself how to play, and often played the game with guests. He had a habit of making up his own rules in order to win. The game he most enjoyed, though, was Parcheesi. His family joked that he was addicted to it. Parcheesi is a pretty simple game, but winning calls for some careful strategy in choosing which pawns to move in order to get all of them home quickly. Being so competitive, Edison enjoyed playing—and winning—a game of strategy like Parcheesi.

Lights, Action, Camera! Edison Makes the Movies

Room 5 in the West Orange laboratory complex remained a mystery for years. No one but Thomas Edison and a few chosen employees were ever allowed to go there, and no one else had a clue as to what they were working on inside. Whatever it was, the project went on quietly for several years. Edison had figured out how to move sound through electrical impulses, such as the telegraph, telephone, and phonograph, but he couldn't hear sounds very well. For Edison, images were important, and he wanted to capture and control images just as he had sound waves. It was not an easy project, but because several inventions came together at once, it was possible.

The Thaumatrope

Toys called thaumatropes were the first "motion pictures." A thaumatrope is made of a round disk with an image on both sides. Two strings are tied to the disk, one held in each hand. When the strings are twisted, then pulled to unwind, the disk rotates quickly, and the images fool the eye into seeing an illusion.

The Zoetrope

Eadweard Muybridge, an English photographer, visited Edison's laboratory in 1886, hoping to find a way to use Edison's phonograph to add sound to his new work on moving images. Muybridge took thousands of photographs of animals as they moved. He captured the movements of galloping horses, flying birds, and even people. He tried to capture movement in a series of photographs snapped quickly one after another. In those days, cameras worked very slowly, so he did

A Short History of Technology, Dover Publications, 1993

A thaumatrope like this was popular in 1826.

MAKE A THAUMATROPE

IN THE EARLY 1800s, Londoners enjoyed twirling the "wonder turner" as they called it, watching as two images merged into one before their eyes. The process is called "persistence of vision," because your eyes and brain think they see one image, but it is actually a blend of two moving images. Persistence of vision means the eye can hold an image for about one twentieth of a second after it disappears. As the images move, the eye interprets them as one continuous motion.

YOU'LL NEED
* Circle, about 3 inches (7.6 cm) across, cut from lightweight cardboard
* Pens or markers
* Hole punch
* 2-foot (61-cm) string

Plan the images first, choosing two things that will blend together in an interesting way. Some thaumatropes had a tree with bare branches on one side of the disk and its leaves on the other. When spinning, it appeared that the leaves were on the branches. The bird-in-a-cage thaumatrope was the most popular. A drawing of a bird was on one side of the disk and a cage on the other—when spinning it looked like the bird was in the cage.

Draw an image on one side of the cardboard circle, then flip the circle over and draw the other image on the back. Flip the circle over so that the top edge of the front drawing will be at the bottom edge of the back drawing. Punch two holes directly across from each other close to the sides of the circle. Tie a 1-foot (61-cm)-long piece of string to

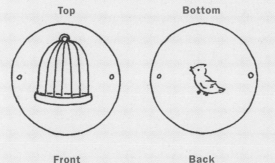

Top   Bottom

Front   Back

each hole by looping it through the hole, slipping the ends through the loop, and pulling tight.

Hold one string in each hand, and rotate one several times to wind up the string. Then gently pull the strings apart as the thaumatrope begins to spin in the center. Watch the image as it spins and enjoy "moving pictures."

The principle of persistence of vision, which fools the eye with quickly changing images, is used to make animation for cartoon videos today. The images change faster than the brain can sort them, so they appear to be in motion.

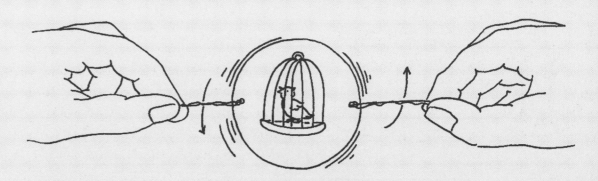

MAKE A FLIP BOOK

A FLIP BOOK is the quickest way to see persistence of vision in action.

YOU'LL NEED
* Several pieces of plain copy paper, 8½ by 11 (21.6 by 28 cm) inches
* Scissors
* Pencil, crayons, markers, or colored pencils
* Stapler

Fold a piece of copy paper in half lengthwise, then in half twice more. Unfold, and you'll have eight rectangles. Cut apart on the folded lines. Make 16 or 20 pieces of paper in this way, all of the same size. Draw an image in the same place on each paper, changing it slightly from one drawing to the next. Some good simple images are flying birds, racing cars, airplanes, or falling stars. Staple the pages together along one edge, then flip the pages quickly to see the image appear to move.

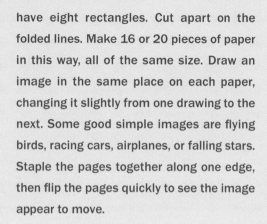

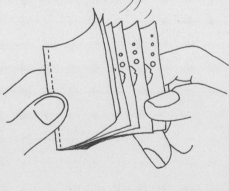

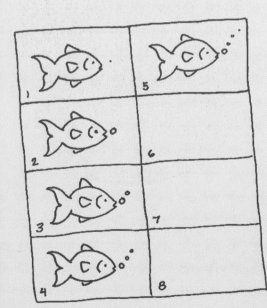

it by using lots of cameras that each took a picture in sequence. He'd done one project taking pictures of racehorses on the track to answer a question that had long been argued: did a galloping horse lift all feet off the ground at once or not? Muybridge's photos proved once and for all that as a horse galloped, all four hooves left the ground.

Muybridge showed Edison his own clever invention, a zoetrope with photographs that appeared to move. As the zoetrope spun around, the photographs appeared in motion. It was clever but nothing really new. The two discussed it, but there didn't seem to be a way to combine the phonograph with the zoetrope—yet. Edison was intrigued but had no quick solution or advice for Muybridge on how to improve the idea. He mulled it over in his head for months, however. Even before he met with Muybridge, Thomas Edison had been thinking about creating a machine that could record and play images, in the way the phonograph could record and play sounds. He wanted to "do for the eye what the phonograph does for the ear," and he began experimenting with making pictures seem to move.

Muybridge didn't invent the zoetrope. It had been invented as an optical illusion toy in the 1830s by William Horner. Because it made simple images appear to come to life with movement, Horner called it the "Wheel of the Devil." When Thomas Edison was a kid, it had become a very popular toy, and the name had changed. The word "zoetrope" comes from two Greek words: *zoa* (living things) and *trope* (turning).

Muybridge rigged a racetrack with strings attached to cameras to capture multiple images, settling once and for all the question of whether all four of a horse's hooves could leave the ground at once.

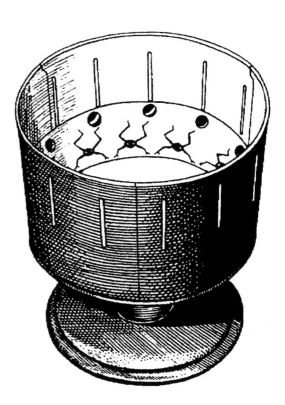

The zoetrope has been called both the "wheel of the devil" and the "wheel of life," because it makes images appear to move.

MAKE A ZOETROPE

A ZOETROPE is a cylinder with a strip of images pasted around the inside. When the cylinder spins, looking through slits at the moving images makes them appear to move. Just like the flip book and the thaumatrope, the principle of persistence of vision is at work. The pictures move so quickly, the eyes can't focus on each one individually, so it appears that the image is in motion. The secret is in making each image slightly different from the one before it.

YOU'LL NEED

* Ruler
* Round cardboard half-gallon (1.9 liter) ice cream container (wash and let dry)
* Scissors
* 8½-by-11-inch (21.6-by-28-cm) sheet of plain white paper
* Tape
* Black pen or marker
* Crayons, markers, or colored pencils
* Glue
* 2 8½-by-11-inch (21.6-by-28-cm) sheets of black construction paper
* Lazy Susan turntable to spin the zoetrope

TO MAKE THE VIEWER

Use a ruler and measure up from the base of the ice cream carton about 3½ inches (8.9 cm).

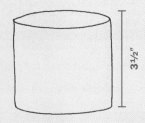

3½"

Trim off the top part of the carton with the scissors, leaving the 3½-inch (8.9-cm)-tall base.

TO MAKE THE PAPER STRIP FOR THE IMAGES

Fold the white paper in thirds lengthwise, then open it up and cut three strips along the creases. Tape two strips together from the back, slightly overlapping. Slide the strip inside the carton and trim to fit so the strip just barely overlaps itself. Take the strip out and fold it in half lengthwise, then in half again, and in half again. Open it up and you will have a strip with eight spaces. Begin drawing in the first space, changing the image slightly in each one that follows. Use the black pen or marker for the drawings and fill in with color if you like. When you're finished, slide the strip inside the container and along the base. Tape or glue it in place.

Cut a strip of black construction paper to measure 6 inches (15.2 cm) wide and about 16 inches (41 cm) long, or long enough to wrap around the outside of the ice cream carton. You may have to tape two pieces of paper together. Make 2-inch (5.1 cm) long slits, about ¼-inch (.63 cm) wide,

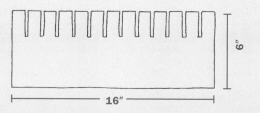

6"

16"

evenly spaced along one long end of the strip. It's easy if you fold the strip in half, in half again, and in half again, measure along the folds, and cut through the folds. Then open up the strip and wrap it around the outside of the carton, with the viewing strips at the top. Tape it securely in place.

You're ready for viewing. Use a couple of pieces of tape to secure the base of the carton to the center of the Lazy Susan, and give it a spin. Position your eyes about a foot away, so you are looking down from the side through the slits. Spinning quickly, the images appear to be moving as you watch. You've fooled your eyes and brain with persistence of vision.

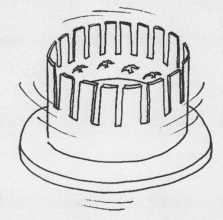

The Kinetoscope

Muybridge's idea of snapping one photograph after another worked to capture figures in motion. But to make a series of images that lasted longer than a few movements would take too many cameras. To photograph a trotting horse for just one minute would take 720 cameras. So, while Muybridge showed that a

This scene shows an attempt to make a kinetoscope and phonograph work together in Edison's Kinetograph.

"Record of a Sneeze" was one of the first moving pictures made in the Edison film lab.

series of photographs could capture movement, his work didn't move beyond that.

After five years' work, Edison's team put together a way to view photographs that seemed more alive than anything done before. They invented a camera that took photographs quickly, one after another, as the subject moved. The photos were printed on long strips of film that were wound around a cylinder that could be turned with a crank. The long flexible filmstrips were the key. Edison hadn't invented the new flexible film—George Eastman (see sidebar at right) was the inventor—but he saw how it could be used to show one image after another. By cutting holes in the sides of the filmstrips, a machine could turn the strips, moving them forward from one scene to the next. In that way, it was a lot like the phonograph, with a cylinder turned by a crank. The strips were inside a viewer, and as you looked through a magnifying glass in the small opening, an electric motor turned the crank and the strip of images flew past, making it seem to come alive. Edison called it the kinetoscope and introduced it in New York City, where it was a hit. Crowds stood in line and paid to view the little moving

← (LEFT) **Thomas Edison with a projecting Kinetoscope made for home use.**

scenes just as they had paid a nickel to put on headphones and listen to the phonograph. The most popular was a 10-round boxing match, which people viewed for one minute each on six consecutive rolls in different machines. They loved it! Police had to be called in to keep order when riots broke out around the boxing show.

Investors bought kinetoscopes and films and set up kinetoscope parlors, like today's video arcades, where customers could move from one machine to another, watching different images, dropping coins in the machine to make it play.

Kinetoscopes were popular, but people wanted to see new scenes, so Edison built a film studio where his crews could shoot more of the short filmstrips. They built a big box-like building, painted black inside and out to make a better background for people and animals in the photographs. They named it the Black Maria. The building had a roof that opened so the sunlight could be adjusted for better photographs. It was also built on a swivel so crews could turn the building to follow the sun and could continue taking photos throughout the day. The swivel feature was probably influenced by Edison's days on the railroad. It was the same technique used in locomotive roundhouses to turn train engines around. Film crews photographed a

GEORGE EASTMAN

|||||||||||||||||||||||||||||||| (1854–1932) ||||||||||||||||||||||||||||||||||

CAMERAS WERE INVENTED long before they could really be useful. Taking pictures required lugging around lots of equipment, glass plates, acid, and other materials. George Eastman, a New York state native, invented a camera named the Kodak, which used film that unrolled on a spool (which he also invented). The name Kodak was created from Eastman's favorite letters of the alphabet and has no real meaning. The Kodak camera was a big seller for decades, and film, which made picture-taking quick, clean, and practical, was the key to its success. Film on a spool also made it possible to create moving pictures, something Thomas Edison quickly realized.

Eastman made a fortune with the Kodak company and gave his money to colleges and universities. He gave away at least $100 million to the University of Rochester, Massachusetts Institute of Technology, Tuskegee Institute, and Hampton Institute. Sometimes he simply signed his gifts under the name "Mr. Smith." In his later years, Eastman suffered from painful arthritis in his back and could barely walk. His health depressed him, and in 1932 at the age of 77, he wrote a note, "My work is done. Why wait?" and shot himself in the heart.

Eastman Kodak Company

wide variety of performers: boxers, dancers, performing dogs, bears, lions, and monkeys.

Watching moving pictures through a peephole was fun for a while, but the novelty soon wore off and customers wanted something better. So did Edison.

The Vitascope

In 1896, Edison's next invention, the Vitascope, made its debut in New York City. The Vitascope was more like today's movie projector—the filmstrip moved through a projector that focused the images upon the wall. It was a hit!

The Vitascope was the end result of years of speculation and work on making moving pictures that could be projected on a wall. For 20 years, many inventors had worked on the idea. Some Kinetoscope parlor owners tried projecting images on the wall so they could charge more customers to watch them. Edison had used some of their ideas, bought patents from others, and added his own ideas. Naturally, he wanted to add sound to the moving images, and with additional work he linked the phonograph to the projected images. But he wasn't able to make the phonograph play at a loud enough volume for a roomful of people sitting far away from it. He put the project aside for the time being and simply added captions to the pictures on the screen. Viewers could read the words that explained what they were seeing. He thought it was fine without sound—after all, he was practically deaf. He said deaf people saw more than others, and he didn't feel anyone else would need the sound to enjoy the images either.

When Edison's team began writing captions that appeared onscreen, they were breaking new ground. No one knew what sort of words or how many would work. They did a lot of experiments with captions. Edison wrote, "We used to experiment with stopwatches on various types of mentalities, trying to strike a fair average of time to all for a given impression to register. We picked children and old persons, clerks, mechanics, business men, professional men, housewives, and exhibited titles with varying numbers of words. When we showed more than six or eight words at a time it was a revelation to see how many failed to get any connected thought at all." Was he right? Some television news shows today crowd the screen with moving images and moving text. Is it hard to follow what the announcer is saying and read the words at the same time? Is there a better way to do it?

Edison was delighted with moving pictures. Although he knew his own success was due to information he'd found in books, he thought that films were actually more educational than books. He experimented with classrooms of children who were taught with films rather than books. They seemed to learn better by seeing rather than reading. "It is my firm conviction that a large part of education in coming generations will be not by books but

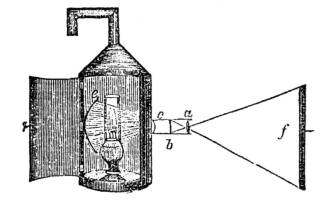

A School Compendium of Natural and Experimental Philosophy, A. S. Barnes & Co., 1858

"Magic Lanterns" like this one had been used since Edison was a boy. An oil lamp inside projected an image through a lens and onto the wall, sort of like today's overhead projector.

by moving pictures," he said. "Children don't need many books when they are shown how to do things. They can learn more by some kinds of moving pictures in five minutes than they can by the usual kind of books in five hours." Today, schools and homes use videos, movies, and DVDs for all sorts of learning. Images really do make learning easier.

Newsreels

The Edison Manufacturing Company made lots of films that were shown in movie theaters around the world. At that time, reading newspapers was the only way to get daily updates on the news. But people wanted to see what was happening for themselves. Movie cameras made it possible to see the people and places the newspaper reporters wrote about. One difficulty was that it was hard for filmmakers to get the "real thing." Early news shows, called "newsreels," sometimes weren't as real as people believed. Most viewers didn't know that the early newsreels were sometimes made at a film studio instead of where the news was happening. Wars were popular newsreel topics, but sometimes the actual scene was too boring or difficult to film. Film crews restaged the battles at home for cameras, and the audience didn't know the difference.

The Spanish-American War in Cuba and the Philippines (1898), the Mexican Revolution (1910), and the Boer War in Africa (1899–1902) were sometimes reenacted by Edison film crews in the Orange Mountains of New Jersey. Men dressed in military uniforms staged battles with each other for the camera but were really members of the New Jersey National Guard. Movie viewers thought they were seeing the "real" thing, but it was actually a "reel" thing!

You can watch some of these films that have been preserved in the Library of Congress. Go online to http://memory.loc.gov/ammem/sawhtml/sawhome.html.

By 1909 there were 8,000 movie theaters across the country. Edison's filming studio was creating longer and more interesting movies. The first feature film, *The Great Train Robbery*, was made at Edison Studios. It is a silent film, before sound was added, but has action scenes of robbers on horseback, fighting men atop train cars that appear to be moving, and plenty of pushing, punching, and brawling. The good guys wear white hats, and the bad guys wear black hats. Audiences loved it. To make the experience even more exciting, theater owners hired organists to play music during the movies, playing fast or slow, loud or soft, to go with whatever was happening onscreen.

The Talkies

Watching moving pictures while reading the words on the screen was fun, but many expected that films would someday be made with sound, too. From the beginning, Edison had tried to combine the phonograph and the moving picture. Finally, in 1900, many years before talkies becme widely available, his team figured out how to make the movies talk. The first demonstration movie included short scenes with sound, showing a person drop-

Edison's film studio, called Black Maria because the inside was painted entirely in black. That made the images photograph better.

ping a china plate on the floor, a man playing a bugle, dogs barking and running around a stage, a politician giving a speech, and several singers. The program ended with "The Star-Spangled Banner." The audience was amazed. It seemed so *real*. But Edison was to turn his own energy elsewhere, leaving the motion picture industry to his employees and the other motion picture inventors and producers who built on his beginnings.

Edison enjoyed creating moving pictures technology, but just as he was having success in that industry he suffered a huge disappointment in his electrical work. He had sold shares in his electrical company, the Edison General Electric Company, to several investors in order to get enough money to support his research on phonograph and motion picture technology. He had let the company's managers build up the business. So it came as a surprise to him when he received the news that the investors had taken over the company and had changed the name to General Electric Company. They had not only moved him out of control in the company, they had removed his name from the company. It was a harsh blow. Edison was very disappointed and for once in his life felt bitterness.

One of Thomas Edison's greatest strengths, however, was his ability to bounce back—to be resilient. Instead of letting bitterness take over his life, or falling into depression, he turned to a new project and vowed it would be a huge success. "I'm going to do something now so different and so much bigger than anything I've ever done before," he said, "people will forget that my name ever was connected with anything electrical."

Houses were one of many things Edison made from concrete.

U.S. Dept. of Interior, National Park Service, Edison National Historic Site.

Always Thinking

Edison Tries New Fields

TURNING AWAY from his film and electrical achievements, Edison really did move into a new field of adventure: large-scale mining. He developed the largest mining equipment at that time and designed systems that gave birth to the American idea of mass production.

Mining was no whim for Edison, who figured he would be able to fill a growing need for iron ore in the United States. Manufacturing was booming, and factories consumed vast amounts of iron ore to build parts for railroads, trains, automobiles, farm equipment, and consumer goods. Yet, just as the nation's industrial production soared, it appeared a shortage of iron ore was about to create problems. Americans wanted to continue making, buying, and selling manufactured goods. Without iron ore, however, they would be without materials, jobs, or the manufactured items that made life more satisfying.

For years, Edison had toyed with the idea of using the magnetic quality of iron ore to improve mining techniques. Back in 1880, he had been visiting a sandy beach on Long Island where he collected some unusual black sand, took it back to the lab, and found it contained iron ore particles. Running a magnet through the sand attracted the ore particles, but not the others, making magnetism an easy way to separate useful iron ore from the sand. Edison knew there were vast amounts of poor quality iron ore scattered in other types of rock. If it could be removed and processed, it would be useful. Because iron ore is attracted to a magnet, Edison figured he could use magnets to pull grains of iron ore sand from crushed rock. He patented a magnetic ore separation process in 1880, and kept thinking about it over the years, jotting ideas and plans in his notebooks.

In 1889 he had time and money to expand on the idea, and he bought up tracts of land in wooded northern New Jersey, where he began mining for iron ore deposits. He and some engineers estimated there were 200 million tons of low-grade iron ore beneath the surrounding 3,000 acres of ground, waiting to be unearthed, crushed into gravel, then separated by the magnetic process. On an additional 16,000 acres, they estimated another 1,000 million tons could be produced. Edison's venture promised to supply America's factories with needed iron ore for the future. "These few acres alone," Thomas Edison said, "contained sufficient ore to supply the whole United States iron trade, including exports, for seventy years."

Not only would he supply America's factories, he would make a large profit. He figured "In six or eight years, I shall take out $10 or $12 million worth of ore a year, at a profit of about $3 million a year clear." After the intense competition and low profits he'd made in electrical systems, mining iron ore seemed like striking gold.

A small town grew up at the mining site, named Edison. The workers lived in company houses that had electricity and running water, designed by Thomas Edison himself. He had a small white-painted house built for his own use when he stayed at the mine during the week. He returned to Glenmont every Saturday night and was back at the mine on Monday morning. Edison spent most of his time at the mine and crusher, enjoying the dust and dirt. The noise didn't bother him at all. He really enjoyed the hard labor—maybe the hard work helped him forget his problems with competitors and investors in the world of manufacturing. He said later, "I never felt better in my life than during the five years I worked here. Hard work, nothing to divert my thoughts, clear air, and simple food made my life very pleasant. We learned a great deal. It will benefit someone some time."

The mine was designed to work differently from other mining operations at the time. Most used men with picks and shovels to mine the rock and horse-drawn wagons to carry the rock and sand. Edison aimed to build an entire operation that eliminated as much hard labor by people as possible. He wanted machines to do the backbreaking

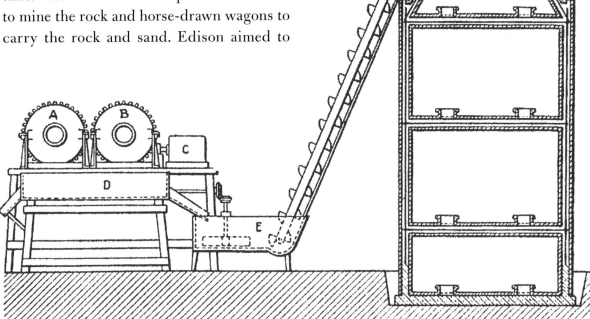

Edison: His Life and Inventions, Harper Brothers, 1910

Edison's ore-crushing operation used the conveyor belt system that was eventually adopted by the rest of industry. It could speed up production while using far less labor. Machines replaced people.

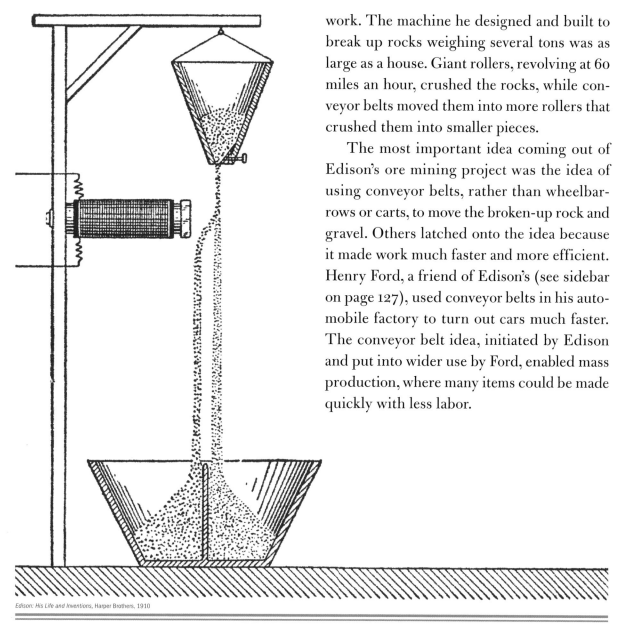

Edison: His Life and Inventions, Harper Brothers, 1910

This is how the magnetic ore separator worked. An electromagnet pulled iron particles from the stream of ground ore.

work. The machine he designed and built to break up rocks weighing several tons was as large as a house. Giant rollers, revolving at 60 miles an hour, crushed the rocks, while conveyor belts moved them into more rollers that crushed them into smaller pieces.

The most important idea coming out of Edison's ore mining project was the idea of using conveyor belts, rather than wheelbarrows or carts, to move the broken-up rock and gravel. Others latched onto the idea because it made work much faster and more efficient. Henry Ford, a friend of Edison's (see sidebar on page 127), used conveyor belts in his automobile factory to turn out cars much faster. The conveyor belt idea, initiated by Edison and put into wider use by Ford, enabled mass production, where many items could be made quickly with less labor.

After passing through several sets of rollers, the fine gravel could be separated with magnets. To do so, the sand passed through the separator, a giant machine that Edison nicknamed the "Ogden Baby." It used 480 magnets to separate out the iron. Conveyor belts moved the iron ore in one direction, and the waste sand off in another. The iron ore was then pressed into briquettes that were shipped to factories where they could be melted down and formed into solid shapes.

The earthmoving equipment, magnetic separator, and crusher all worked just fine, and Edison thought he'd solved the national iron ore shortage. He hoped to recover the large amount of money he'd invested in setting up his huge operation, as well as the money he had lost when General Electric was formed.

Just as he was settling into the idea of success, news came from northern Minnesota that ended the entire operation. Geologists had discovered new deposits of high-quality iron ore in the Mesabi mountains of Minnesota. It was cheaper to ship ore from Minnesota across the Great Lakes than to crush and process rocks for ore. The new deposits were so large and easy to ship, the price of iron ore dropped from $6 a ton to $4 a ton, and Edison was forced to close the ore mining operation because he couldn't cover his expenses.

He had lost a lot of money on the venture—$2 million—but as usual he was still optimistic. "Well, it's all gone," Edison told an employee. "But we had a hell of a good time spending it." Even if he lost all his money, he said, he could always return to a job as a telegrapher if he had to. Edison's spirit was never diminished. When others considered a project a failure, Edison claimed that at least some knowledge was gained from every experience. His mining operation showed that he was correct about separating ore with magnets, and his idea of conveyor belts made industrial work much more efficient.

MAKE A MAGNETIC SEPARATOR

SOME MINERALS have magnetic properties and others don't. You can make a simple separator to sort two minerals, like Edison did. You'll use iron and sodium.

YOU'LL NEED
* Iron filings—about 1 teaspoon (from a machine shop or hardware or educational supply stores. See the Resources section of this book)
* Salt (about 1 teaspoon)
* Plastic sandwich bag
* Bar magnet (any size)

Put the filings and salt in a plastic bag and shake it to mix the two minerals completely. Empty the contents of the bag onto a tabletop. Slowly lower the magnet to the minerals, watching to see if the magnetic force pulls filings up from the table to the magnet. Magnetic force is stronger than gravity. The salt will remain on the table, but the iron will cling to the magnet. Keep working until you have separated all the iron from the salt.

Why does it work? The iron is made of iron atoms that are attracted to the magnet, while the salt is made of sodium and chlorine, and neither element is attracted to a magnet.

You can try other materials, too. One interesting experiment is to place half a box of Total brand cereal in a blender, add water to cover, and blend thoroughly. Pour the mixture into a glass bowl, and run a bar magnet through the slush. Iron filings will appear on the magnet. The iron was added to the cereal, along with other supplements, to make the cereal more nutritious.

MAKE AN ELECTROMAGNET

TAKE THE MAGNET experiment a bit further by making your own electromagnet. It's better than a bar magnet because you can turn the magnetization on and off by connecting to an electrical charge from a battery. That's how Edison could turn his iron separator on and off, and its also how coin-operated vending machines work. The coin trips an electromagnet, making a connection that causes the machine to dispense an item. Electromagnets are used a lot today, in things like bells and buzzers, too.

YOU'LL NEED

* 3 feet (.91 m) of bell wire (copper wire with an insulated covering, available at hardware stores)
* Large nail
* Scissors
* Tape
* C-cell flashlight battery
* Thumbtacks, paper clips, sewing pins, or safety pins—anything light and made of metal

Wrap the bell wire around the center of the nail, leaving about 6 inches (15.2 cm) of wire extended at both ends of the nail. Keep the wrapped wire tight as you move down the nail. Trim away the plastic insulator covering at both ends of the wire by scoring gently with the scissors, then pulling the covering off with your fingernails. There should be about ½ inch (1.3 cm) of uncovered wire at each end.

Tape the battery to the table, so it won't roll while you're working. Holding onto the plastic-covered wire, touch the bare ends of wire to each end of the battery. Don't touch the uncovered wire because it will get hot as the current passes through. Lay some metal objects, such as thumbtacks or paper clips, on the table, and move the nail toward them. The nail will attract the objects. When you disconnect the wire at either end of the battery you will break the circuit, end the magnetic effect of the nail, and release the paper clip. The secret to the magnetic effect is the way the wire is coiled next to itself.

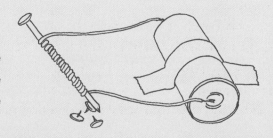

Edison Cement

Even though he'd spent lots of time and money developing the ore operation, Edison closed it down. Looking for another way to use both his expensive machinery and his new knowledge of geology, Thomas Edison found another opportunity.

In 1898, just as Edison's iron mining venture collapsed, cement rock was discovered in New Village, about 45 miles (72.4 km) from West Orange. Edison jumped at the chance to shift his attention to something new: making cement. It was a way to make use of his knowledge about rocks and put his expensive ore-grinding machinery back to work. Cement was just beginning to get attention as a building material in the United States, as the era of bridge and canal building began.

Cement had been developed by the Romans centuries earlier, but the techniques for making it had been forgotten. Roman builders had mixed together water, crushed limestone, and volcanic ash to build canals, aqueducts, buildings, and the Forum. The structures still stood, but the secrets behind building them had disappeared.

In the 1700s an Englishman named John Smeaton studied the works of Vitruvius, a Roman writer who told about the ancient builders. He found that they had used a special limestone rock from Italy that hardened underwater. He used the idea to build a lighthouse off the coast of Cornwall, in a spot that was difficult because it was partially submerged in water. It was so successful that wooden lighthouses soon became a thing of the past, as cement structures took their place.

In the early 1800s, Canvas White, a New York state resident, discovered that certain rock could be heated, ground up, and then mixed with water to make a hard compound. He patented the idea and sold his cement to the builders of the Erie Canal, which connects the Great Lakes and the Atlantic Ocean.

Edison's cement plant operation was huge, with machines larger than anyone had used before. He was the first to use the steam shovel to dig large amounts of rock from the ground, pulling up five-ton chunks in one scoop. He used a small railroad to bring cars loaded with rock up from the depths of the mining pit. He designed a 150-foot-long (46 m) rotating kiln in which the limestone rock could be heated to high temperatures. Then it was ground into fine dust in a new type of roller crusher. His equipment was powered by electricity, making it powerful and efficient. He contributed many innovations that made the cement industry more efficient: scales to weigh rock, equipment to bag the dry cement, conveyor belts to move bags and rock between machines, and dozens of more ideas.

Edison discovered that chemistry was at the heart of successful cement production because the proportions of silica, calcium, iron, aluminum, and limestone had to be exactly the same in every batch of cement. When cement hardens, it isn't because the water has evaporated but because the water caused a chemical reaction that made the materials firm. Different rocks and gravels contain different chemicals, so lab testing was done at the quarry to determine the proportions of raw materials. Wrong amounts in the mixture can make the finished product weak and crumbly instead of hard and strong.

Concrete, made by adding sand to the cement mixture, could be poured into molds or frames to make nearly any kind of structure. It was strong, fireproof, never needed painting, and lasted for centuries. Best of all, it wasn't very expensive. Edison tried making many different things from concrete, including phonograph cabinets, pianos, and bedroom furniture.

The Edison Portland Cement Company made cement for use in concrete structures such as dams, apartment buildings, hotels, schools, roads, and canals. But it was cement houses that Edison thought would be most

The Romance of Cement, Edison Company, 1926

Concrete made a great material for building lighthouses. It was strong enough to resist dampness and waves.

PLASTER OF PARIS HAND CAST

PLASTER OF PARIS hardens in a similar way to cement. It works by a chemical reaction when water is added to the chalky dust. Here's a simple project that lets you watch the liquid turn to solid. Be sure to work outdoors, and do not pour any of the plaster and water mixture down the sink. It will harden and clog the drain.

YOU'LL NEED
* Old newspapers
* 3 cups (710 ml) of Plaster of Paris, available at art and craft supply stores
* Empty paper milk carton (rinse out and open the top)
* 2 cups (473 ml) of water
* Paint stirring stick (free at stores that sell paint)
* Disposable aluminum pie plate
* Vaseline or salad oil
* Small pebbles or marbles (optional)
* Tempera paints (optional)

Cover your work surface with the old newspapers. Put 3 cups (710 ml) of dry plaster into the milk carton. Slowly add the water, stirring with the stirring stick until all the powder dissolves. When the mixture is smooth, pour it into the aluminum pie plate. Cover your hand with Vaseline or salad oil, and when the mixture begins to get solid, press your hand into the plaster. Hold it still for a few minutes, then remove your hand. Did you feel the warmth of the plaster as it hardened? That's because a chemical reaction between the dry materials and the water is taking place, which makes them harden into a solid. The same thing happens when concrete becomes solid.

You can make interesting wall plaques by pressing small pebbles into the plaster before it hardens. To make colored plaster, add tempera paint to the wet mixture before it hardens. Concrete can be tinted different colors, too.

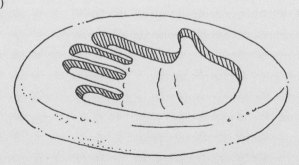

useful to people. He figured the houses could be made by pouring cement into a mold, so they would be inexpensive to build. Also, they would last and never burn down, so there would be no expenses for repairs or fire insurance. In 1910 Edison built two concrete buildings at Glenmont: a gardener's cottage and a garage. He welcomed others to use the idea, too, in order to create inexpensive houses to fill the needs of poor people crammed in city tenements. "I have not gone into this with the idea of making money from it," he said, "and will be glad to license reputable parties to make molds and erect houses without any payments on account of patents. The only restriction being that the designs of the houses be satisfactory to me, and that they shall use good material."

Edison built several dozen concrete houses. Once the molds were assembled, it took only six hours to pour the concrete for a two-story house. The total cost to build a concrete house was about $1,200. Edison thought even inexpensive houses should be as nice as possible, so he created a house with front and back porches, four bedrooms, a parlor, and cellar. Even the bathroom furnishings were poured in concrete. The molds could be rearranged for each house so they didn't all look alike.

But the molds presented a problem. It took about 2,300 different pieces to mold a house, and it would cost builders about $175,000 to get started with a set of molds. That was such a large investment that no one was interested.

Some of Edison's concrete houses still exist in Ohio and New Jersey. In Newark, Ohio, a couple living in one reports they love their two-story, four-bedroom house. Their only complaint is that it's hard to drive nails into the concrete walls to hang pictures.

Edison loved making things from concrete and thought up many projects that might be made from the almost magical material. His houses didn't become popular; neither did the phonograph cabinets he designed to be molded in concrete. Perhaps he was ahead of his time—concrete construction, reinforced with pieces of steel rebar, later became popular in large commercial buildings and projects.

Edison's cement company did supply 180,000 bags of cement to build Yankee Stadium in New York City, and most of the Panama Canal was built with Edison's cement. More recent examples of concrete construction are Trump Tower and Trump World Tower. The Trump World Tower is 860 feet (262 m) tall, the tallest reinforced concrete building in New York City.

To continue building and marketing concrete houses would have taken a large investment of time and money, and Edison was not inclined to do that. Instead, he lost interest and returned to other inventions. His concrete company continued, however, quite successfully in the 1920s, but closed during the Great Depression of the 1930s.

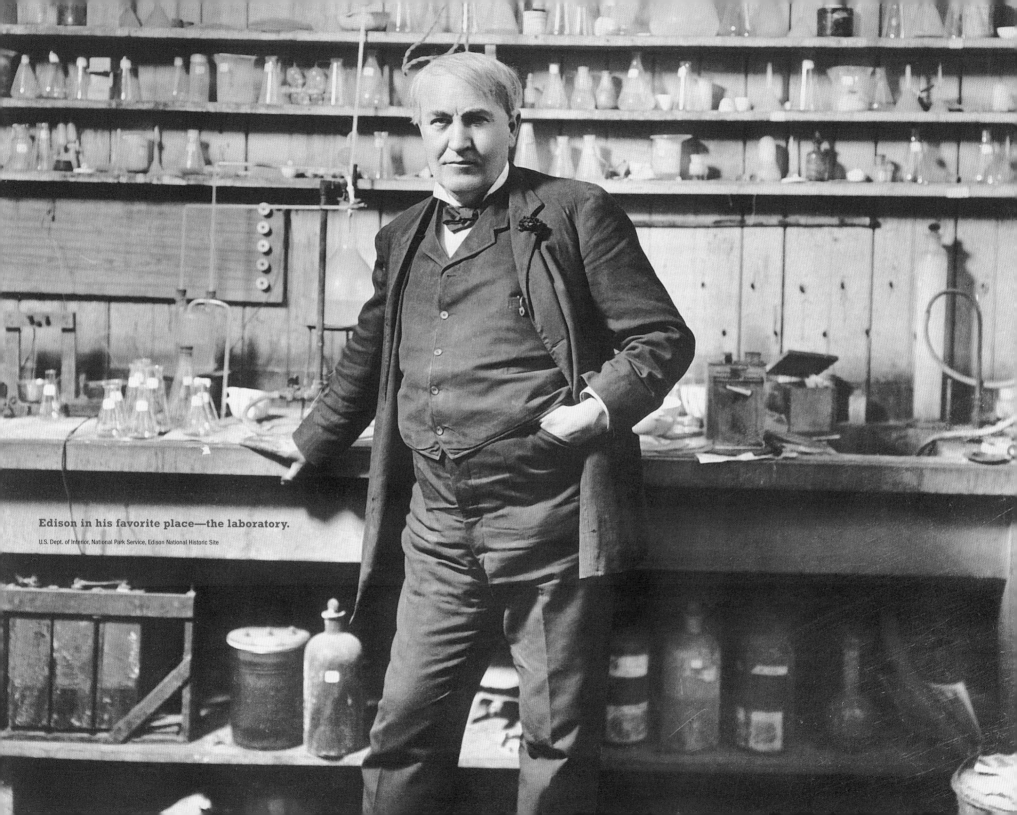

Edison in his favorite place—the laboratory.

8

Successes and Setbacks

> "WE SOMETIMES LEARN A LOT FROM OUR FAILURES IF WE HAVE PUT INTO THE EFFORT THE BEST THOUGHT AND WORK WE ARE CAPABLE OF."
> —THOMAS EDISON

A Long Career as an Inventor

TIMES WERE CHANGING in the early 20th century. The Edison family had grown, with the birth of three children to Thomas and Mina: Madeleine, Charles, and Theodore. Glenmont was full, and the West Orange workshops were bustling. Edison tried to give more attention to the younger children than he had his older ones, who claimed their father had never been there for them. His work had always come first. Now that he was in his 60s and even more successful, he spent Sundays with the family more frequently.

Even though Edison devoted more time to his family, he was as productive as ever. He continued with many experiments and projects. Many of Edison's projects took years to develop, and that meant work overlapped with other, often unrelated projects.

The X-Ray

Moving pictures allowed people to watch the human body in action. Now Thomas Edison saw an opportunity to do something he'd

Smithsonian Institution, 87-1626

Florida State Archives

⭧ (ABOVE) **Edison reading a book in the yard of his New Jersey home.** ⭠ (LEFT) **Thomas Edison with his wife, Mina, and the children.**

wanted to do for a long time: look *inside* the human body. When Edison was young, he experimented with electrical charges by working on batteries and telegraphs, but he also experimented with something new at the time: the idea of using electricity to cure disease. Healers treated patients with electrical charges passed through wires that touched against their head or parts of the body that were in pain.

Edison had participated in electrical healing, too, which is not surprising due to his lifelong interest in electricity. While growing up, Edison discovered how to use electrically charged wires to pass weak electrical charges from a battery and was often paid to help sick people. He performed "electric treatments" using wires attached to a telegraph battery. In one instance, a girl had fallen on the ice and was unconscious. The doctor, unable to revive her, sent for young Edison, who held the wire in one hand while massaging the girl's head with the other. She revived!

Edison had often tinkered with ideas to use electricity to cure disease, so when Wilhelm Roentgen, a German scientist, discovered how radiation could light up the bones inside the body in 1895, Edison was interested. Roentgen had used a high-voltage electric current and a vacuum tube to shine a light on his wife's hand. It revealed the bones inside

her hand on a photographic plate. The tube used radium, a radioactive metal found in uranium, to light up an object. After reading the news story, Edison urged his employees to drop everything and concentrate on developing this new idea. He already knew a lot about passing light through a glass vacuum tube—that's what a light bulb was. The dif-

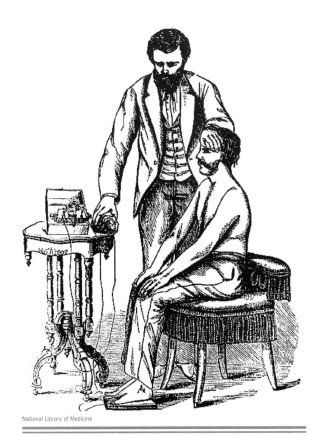

A doctor uses electricity to treat a patient. Electric current is still used in some medical treatments today.

ference with an x-ray tube is that the electrically heated filament emits electrons that strike a metal plate and emit short wavelength radiation. It didn't take Thomas Edison long to use Roentgen's ideas to create a radium light bulb. It burned nicely, but when a lab assistant working on the project lost all his hair and his skin developed sores, others refused to work on the project and Edison dropped the idea. His assistant, Clarence Dally, soon showed worse effects from the exposure to radiation. He had to have both hands, then arms, amputated to stop disease from spreading, and he died a few years later. Edison, too, suffered damage to his eyes, which later healed. At the time, no one realized they should protect themselves from x-ray damage. Today, technicians and patients use lead drapes and shields to block damaging radiation during x-ray procedures.

Edison wanted to develop Roentgen's discovery into technology that could be useful, and he knew from the start that it would be a useful way for doctors to look inside the body. Still, it took experiments with 8,000 different compounds to find calcium tungstate, which produced a clear image when struck by x-rays. Using this, Edison created the fluoroscope, which was a viewing screen where the x-ray images could be examined.

The fluoroscope was powered by electricity and lit up the inside of people's bodies on a screen so they could see their bones. It was a huge hit at the 1896 Electrical Exhibition in New York City, where thousands of people passed in front of Edison's fluoroscope machine to see their own bones. Using designs from his earlier work on the Kinetoscope, Edison made the peephole fluoroscope, which one looked into to see the x-ray image. Physicians quickly called on Edison to help them use the new technology with patients. Edison didn't patent the fluoroscope. He thought it should be freely available so doctors could use x-rays to help save lives.

In 1901, after the device had been on the market for five years, an assassin shot President William McKinley. The president's doctors called Edison to send a fluoroscope, which he did. After the equipment arrived, however, the doctors thought McKinley was recovering and that it was too dangerous to try removing the bullet from his body. They decided not to use the x-ray. McKinley's condi-

THE BODY ELECTRIC

TINY ELECTRICAL CHARGES move continually through the human heart, making it beat regularly. The impulses travel through the tissues out to the skin, where they can be detected. That makes it possible to use a device wrapped around your arm to measure the heart's rhythm in an electrocardiogram test.

tion grew worse, and he died. While the x-ray didn't save McKinley's life, it has helped doctors treat people for the past century. It was the basis for today's medical x-ray technology, as well as security x-ray machines used in airports. But not everyone thought it was a good idea. One newspaper said it was a terrible idea to look at people's bones, that it was repulsive and indecent, and called for laws to make it illegal. The writer said, "Perhaps the best thing may be for all civilized nations to combine to burn all works on the Roentgen Ray, to execute the discoverers and to corner all the tungstate in the world and throw it in the middle of the ocean. Let the fish contemplate each other's bones if they like."

Thulesius

In 1896, Edison's fluoroscope allowed a look at the bones inside the human body.

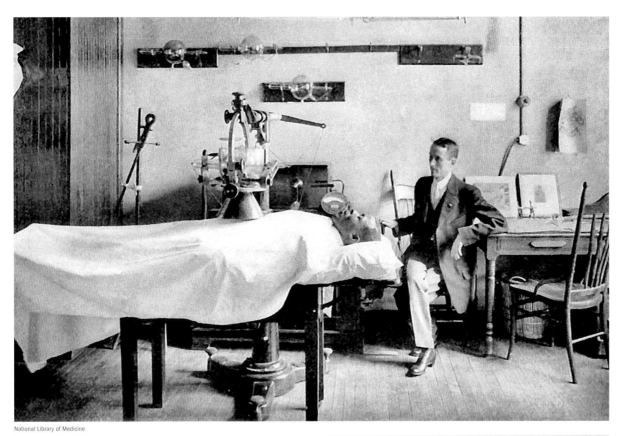

National Library of Medicine

One of the first hospital x-ray departments, at Central Dispensary and Emergency Hospital, Washington, DC.

Edison Improves the Automobile Battery

It wasn't long before Edison was immersed in another project that he felt would change the lives of Americans, like the light bulb, the phonograph, and moving pictures had. In 1907, Henry Ford (see sidebar on page 127) perfected an automobile that went 20 miles on a gallon of fuel. It cost only $600, which was remarkable because until then most automobiles had been made as amusements for the wealthy. Ford's factory in Detroit began turning out hundreds, then thousands, of low-priced vehicles that ordinary Americans could afford.

Automobiles were invented in Europe and were designed with engines that ran on a variety of fuels: steam, vegetable oil, alcohol, kerosene, and electricity. Because Edison hated horses (and their smelly manure) on city streets, he welcomed automobiles and looked forward to the day when they would replace horses on public roadways. But automobiles had their drawbacks too; Edison didn't like the smoky fumes the new machines put out. To him, clean, quiet, electric-powered automobiles made sense. Electric cars were very popular in cities. In New York City in 1899 there were about 100 taxicabs—90 of them powered by electric batteries. They were quieter than steamers and more reliable than gas cars, which didn't work very well. But no one had been able to create electric automobiles that could travel long distances, because the electricity had to be stored in a battery, and batteries were heavy and didn't stay charged for very long. This created a perfect challenge for Edison, who said, "I guess I'll have to make a battery."

From the time he was a child, Edison had worked with batteries, trying to improve them. Invented in the 19th century, batteries were made from lead and filled with sulphuric acid. The more energy one wanted from a battery, the larger and heavier it had to be. Now Edison dreamed of creating a small, portable battery that would make electric cars more practical. He called it a "box of electricity." Edison spent long hours experimenting in the lab. Sometimes he worked through the night, stopping only for catnaps or meals sent by his wife. He and his team tried over 9,000 experiments. After several years' work, Edison and his staff (90 people worked on the project) succeeded in making a smaller, lighter battery that could power vehicles longer than the older-style batteries.

The new battery had very thin plates of nickel, a much lighter substance than the iron or lead used in older batteries. The new bat-

FLYING HIGH

EDISON EXPERIMENTED with making a flying machine. In 1885, he tried to design a helicopter, building a model that burned paper as fuel. It didn't work, and during testing Edison and an employee were badly burned. Edison said, "You've got to have a machine heavier than air and then find something to lift it with. That's the trouble, though, to find the *something*. I may find it one of these days." Edison was thrilled in 1903 when the Wright brothers successfully flew their airplane. He knew it would be the transportation mode of the future.

tery was used to power a test vehicle that could go 100 miles on a charge. Edison's batteries were tested at the lab by shaking them up and down with machines, and by dropping them from a third-floor window. Edison wanted a durable battery that would take the rough treatment America's rocky roads gave the early automobiles.

In 1904, Edison set up a factory at Silver Lake, New Jersey, and hired 450 workers to manufacture his new batteries. He had more orders from automakers than the factory could fill. But batteries could do more than power cars. Large batteries could also be recharged with a gasoline-powered engine, and then used to light and heat homes and barns. For rural homes, far from power lines to connect to central power sources, the battery brought electricity within reach. Edison told newspaper reporters, "I hope that the time has nearly arrived when every man may not only be able to light his own house, but charge his own machinery, heat his rooms, cook his food, etc., by electricity, without depending on anyone else for these services."

Soon, however, reports began trickling into the factory that the batteries weren't working as well as they were supposed to. They lost power, they leaked, and the electrical contacts weren't working properly. Edison knew it would take a complete redesign of the

battery to improve its flaws, which would be a tremendous expense. It was tempting to continue making and selling the batteries—for a while anyway—but Edison resisted. There was nothing he wanted more than public approval, and he had given the public a product that didn't work. He ordered a halt to

Thomas Edison and his wife, Mina, enjoy her electric automobile.

MAKE YOUR OWN BATTERY TESTER

BATTERIES lose the electrical charge they hold over time and use, one of the main problems Edison had with his first version of the storage battery. How can you tell if a battery still has electrical energy stored inside, or if it needs to be replaced or recharged? You can't tell by looking at it or weighing it, you must check the electrical charge. Make this simple device to test batteries around the house.

YOU'LL NEED
* Scissors
* 6 inches (15.2 cm) of bell wire (plastic covered copper wire)
* Tape (plastic electrical tape is best, but masking tape will work)
* Small light bulb
* Several household batteries

Use the scissors to score and pull away about ½ inch (1.3 cm) of plastic covering on the ends of the wire. Tape one end of the wire to the side of the metal socket at the base of the light bulb. To test the battery, touch the bare end of the wire to the base of the battery, and the metal part of the light bulb socket to the top of the battery. If there is enough electricity to make a current, the light will turn on. If the light doesn't go on, there probably isn't any electricity left in the battery. Your tester can be useful if something battery-powered, such as a flashlight, isn't working. You can test the batteries in the flashlight to see whether they still have a charge. If they do, perhaps the flashlight itself needs repair.

the manufacturing of more batteries and recalled all those that had been sold.

Edison didn't call anything a failure. Instead, he knew that if an experiment or project didn't work out, it only revealed what wouldn't work—the solution was still to be discovered. For example, during Edison's work on the battery, a visitor found him at a workbench one night with hundreds of chemical samples before him for testing. The visitor said, "Isn't it a shame that with the tremendous amount of work you have done you haven't been able to get any results?" Edison smiled and said, "Results! Why, man, I have gotten a lot of results! I know several thousand things that won't work!"

Edison said, "In trying to perfect a thing, I sometimes run straight up against a granite wall a hundred feet high. If, after trying and trying and trying again, I can't get over it, I turn to something else. Then, someday, it may be months or it may be years later, something is discovered either by myself or someone else, or something happens in some part of the world, which I recognize may help me to scale at least part of that wall."

Edison put the entire laboratory to work on improving the battery, using money made from the movie *The Great Train Robbery*, which was a national hit. It took five more years and 10,296 experiments to perfect the battery. By the time it was finished, it had taken Edison 10 years total, and he was beginning to age. He was pale, his thick hair turning white.

After Edison perfected the battery, electric cars and delivery trucks became very popular in cities. Women especially liked the clean,

The Country Gentleman, September 28, 1918

↞ (LEFT) This advertisement for Edison's storage battery showed how farm families could use it to power lights and equipment on the farm. They could enjoy electricity without being connected to power lines from a distant power source. ↟ (ABOVE) This Seattle woman enjoys an electric automobile.

quiet, electric automobiles, which could now travel 60 miles (96 km) before needing to be recharged and were fully charged after being plugged in for seven hours. After World War I began, however, vehicles powered by petroleum gasoline became so common that the electric car faded away until the end of the 20th century, when high petroleum prices led inventors to come up with the hybrid vehicle that combines electricity from a battery with a gasoline engine.

Edison's battery wasn't useless, however. Even if a vehicle has a gasoline-powered engine, it still needs a battery to start the engine. Instead of starting the engine with a hand crank, as the early gasoline vehicles did, the battery sparks a flame that ignites the gasoline in the engine. Auto batteries also run the other equipment in the car, such as headlights and radio. The improved battery was important in making gasoline-fueled vehicles that worked successfully.

The Automatic Store

Among Edison's many ideas was one he called "the clerkless shop." He predicted that in the future, people would shop at stores where they bought items from boxes in the walls. They would insert coins in a slot and receive the item they wanted. It was a very unusual idea when he described it in 1910. Stores then were not even self-serve; the shopkeeper kept items in glass cases and on shelves behind the cash register. The shopkeeper had to weigh or measure and cut whatever amount of an item the shopper wanted to buy. Products weren't packaged; they were in barrels and bins. To think a store would operate with people helping themselves to selections in slot machines seemed so unreal that the story took up an entire page in the *New York Times*. Edison explained that the machines would work by electromagnets that opened chutes to let items drop down to the opening where the customer could reach them. He said there would be dozens of openings, labeled with signs in half a dozen languages telling what article was for sale behind the little door.

He thought the automatic store would be good for poor people—merchandise could be priced lower because there was no need to pay so many clerks. Store owners would also benefit because all their sales would be in cash. In those days storekeepers sold items on credit to most customers and sometimes lost money when the customers didn't pay their bills.

Edison moved on to other ideas, but eventually vending machines became the sort of "automatic store" he predicted.

"You'll Never See a Fire Like This Again!"

Thomas Edison had many setbacks in his life but always overcame them with good spirits and pushed on. In 1914, just as World War I began in Europe, Edison's laboratory caught fire.

Things began with a big explosion in the film laboratory in the West Orange, New Jersey, factory. It's still not clear how it started, but the explosion set the entire building on fire and the huge amount of chemicals kept on hand for experimenting and production quickly ignited. By the time firemen arrived on the scene, several buildings were ablaze. Edison was on hand, directing firefighters while jotting down notes in a small notebook. He was making notes for the rebuilding project he would start the next day. When his son Charles ran up, he told the boy to run home and get his mother and the other children. "They'll never see a fire like this again!" he said.

The firemen fought the blaze in spite of darkness, cold weather, and bursts of snow. In the end, 10 buildings—three-fourths of the entire complex—were destroyed. During the fire, Edison, his wife, and employees dragged out pieces of furniture, statues, equipment,

Edison in the laboratory.

phonographs, and whatever they could save. But much was lost, including several glass jars in the phonograph building that were filled with diamonds used to etch recordings on phonograph records.

Later, as Edison was digging in the rubble, he was pleased to find a framed photograph of himself that hadn't been destroyed. The glass was cracked and the frame blackened, but he saved it and wrote: "Never touched me" on it. He told reporters the next morning that, "Although I am over 67 years old, I'll start over again tomorrow." And he did. Within months everything was back in business. And, always watching for how he could make things that helped people, Edison invented a battery-powered searchlight to make it easier for firefighters working in darkness and smoke.

Hiring the Best and Brightest

Many people wanted to work in Edison's labs and workshops, but because most of the things they would be doing on the job hadn't even been thought of yet, choosing employees was hard. Edison wondered how to select people who were intelligent, cooperative, and creative. One could test whether a person knew math, but there was no way to tell if that person could invent.

Sometimes Edison tested a job applicant by pointing toward a pile of equipment and telling the applicant to assemble it and get it running. When someone succeeded, he hired that person immediately. Another story is that when Edison was about to hire a new employee, he would invite the applicant over for a bowl of soup. If the person salted the soup before tasting it, Edison wouldn't offer him the job. He thought salting before tasting might mean the person made too many assumptions. He wanted workers who challenged assumptions.

In 1920, Edison made up written exams to give job applicants to see if they had the right qualities. The tests were copied on the mimeograph machine (which he had invented earlier) and included 150 different questions. The job applicants had two hours to fill in answers in the space below each question. The questions were about technical knowledge, like chemistry, or mathematical puzzles. Some questions were tricky, including one, for example, about poker. The answer Edison was looking for was: "I don't play poker."

Did the tests help Edison pick the best employees? He thought so. Those he hired who had scored well on the tests turned out to be good employees. He said the few he had hired without having administered the test turned out to be poor workers. Edison graded the tests himself. Only 6 percent of those who took the test got As and were hired. That would be only six test takers out of every 100.

At first, people didn't accept the idea of giving tests as a way to pick the best person for a job. Edison was criticized and ridiculed for giving the tests. An article in the *New York Times* said, "He may enjoy a brief triumph with his catch questions, but he cannot grade the human soul." Test takers were asked to keep the questions secret, but two men took the test to the *New York Times* newspaper, which published 146 test questions and answers thought to be correct. What did Thomas Edison do? He created new tests. He knew that having a college degree didn't mean a person had wide general knowledge, which came from reading a lot of books. People who did well on his tests were those who had read a wide variety of books. One of his own sons, Charles, after graduating with a degree from the Massachusetts Institute of Technology, couldn't pass the test.

Despite the critics, testing became more popular. Today, job applicants are tested on many subjects, even on their personality.

TAKE EDISON'S TEST

THESE ARE QUESTIONS test takers remembered from Edison's tests. Take the test and check your answers.

How did you do? You can take a longer version of the test online and learn your score immediately. Go to the Edison National Historic Web site, operated by the National Park Service, at www.nps.gov/edis/edifun/quiz/quiz_launch.htm. If you get an A on that test, you'll get a pretend job interview with Thomas Edison. Good luck!

1. **What countries bound France?**
2. **What country produces the finest china?**
3. **Where is the Volga River?**
4. **What is celluloid made from?**
5. **What country consumed the most ice before the war?**
6. **What city in the U.S. leads in making laundry machines?**
7. **Who invented the cotton gin?**
8. **What country is the greatest textile producer?**
9. **Is Australia larger than Greenland in area?**
10. **Where is Copenhagen?**
11. **Who discovered radium?**
12. **Where is platinum found?**
13. **What is artificial silk made from?**
14. **What are violin strings made of?**
15. **Who was Bessemer and what did he do?**
16. **Name three principal alkalis.**
17. **What is copra?**
18. **Who discovered the Pacific Ocean?**
19. **What causes the ocean tides?**
20. **What is the capital of Alabama?**

ANSWERS

1. Spain, Andorra, Monaco, Italy, Switzerland, Germany, Luxemburg, and Belgium 2. Limoges, France, or Dresden, Germany 3. Russia 4. Wood pulp 5. Russia 6. Chicago 7. Eli Whitney 8. Great Britain, with U.S. close second 9. Trick question! Australia is three times larger than Greenland, but because Mercator maps distort the size of the continents, Greenland looks larger on maps. 10. Denmark 11. Madame Curie 12. Ural Mountains between Europe and Asia 13. Cotton or wood pulp treated with acids 14. Catgut, which is sheep's intestines 15. English engineer who invented steelmaking process that took carbon out of molten iron with blasts of air 16. Soda, potash, ammonia 17. Dried coconut fiber 18. Balboa 19. Gravitational pull of the moon 20. Montgomery

Thomas Edison with John Burroughs (center)
and Henry Ford (right).

Plants, Friendship, and Rubber

9

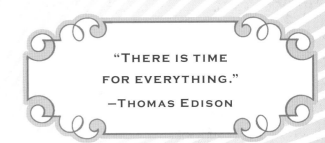

Edison's Final Years

MANY PEOPLE don't realize that Thomas Edison spent much of his adult life in Florida. For nearly 50 years, he kept a house and laboratory in the western Florida Everglades, visiting often and spending many winters in the sunny climate. In the early years, when the children were babies and toddlers, the Edisons stayed in New Jersey rather than make the long trip to Florida, but as the children grew older Florida became a longed-for escape from New Jersey winters. Even when he was busy with projects, Edison found he needed to escape from the pressure in the New Jersey labs. After 1901, the family enlarged their Florida home and began spending every winter there.

Enjoying Friendship and Nature

Henry Ford, who eventually became the world's most successful and famous automobile manufacturer, became Thomas Edison's closest friend. The two first met when Ford was working as a mechanic for the Edison Illuminating Company of Detroit (later renamed Detroit Edison) in the 1880s. They both attended a company banquet, where someone pointed Ford out to Edison, saying, "There's a young fellow who has made a gas car." Edison was impressed. The two men began chatting about automobile design and engines, and Edison, who was older, famous, and successful by that time, told Ford to keep up the work. He slammed his fist on the table and told him, "You have the thing—keep at it!" That encouragement fired young Henry Ford's enthusiasm and kept him inspired for years. Edison liked Ford immensely. He liked Ford's brilliant mind and passion for inventing. The two were very much alike. Neither had gone to college, and both had come from small Michigan towns. "This fellow Ford is like the postage stamp," Edison said about his friend. "He sticks to one thing until he gets there."

During the years Edison worked on the storage battery project, he invited Henry Ford, by then a very successful automobile manufacturer, to visit the New Jersey laboratory to discuss whether Edison could produce batteries for Ford's cars. The two became close friends after that, and began going on automobile drives in the country and on camping trips. They invited along one of Ford's idols, John Burroughs, a famous naturalist. Burroughs had written books about nature and birds, and Henry Ford loved birds so much he had 500 birdhouses installed on his farm in Michigan. The three men got along well and took summer camping trips together around the country. Harvey Firestone, a successful tire manufacturer, joined them. Because Edison, Ford, Burroughs, and Firestone were famous men, their camping trips made the news. Sometimes crews of newspaper reporters followed them.

The group tramped through the Great Smoky Mountains, the Adirondacks, the Everglades, the Big Cyprus Swamp, and New England. They said they were traveling into "nature's laboratory." The new technology of the automobile, which all but Burroughs had played a part in, made it possible to travel so far and so often. The automobile was opening up the back roads and nature study to the rest of America, too, as people began driving just to see and appreciate natural beauty. While walking through woods and forests, Edison collected cuttings and seeds from plants he wanted to try growing in his gardens to create raw materials for future experiments.

Edison enjoyed nature, but he liked the friendship and fun the trips provided even more. Edison liked the storytelling and joking the most. While Ford and Burroughs did serious bird-watching, Edison told jokes like this one: "A gorgeous bird is the pelican, whose bill can hold more than his bellican, he can put in his beak, food enough for a week, but I'm blest if I can see how in hellican."

His friends described Edison on these camping trips as "a good camper, he turns vagabond very easily, can go with his hair disheveled and clothes unbrushed as long as the best of us and can rough it week in and week out and wear his benevolent smile." In the 1920s, President Warren Harding joined the camping party, followed later by President Calvin Coolidge. Eventually the trips faded away because they attracted too many reporters and the famous campers couldn't have any privacy.

The Edison and Ford families got along so well that Henry Ford decided to buy the house next door to the Edisons' winter home in Florida. Now neighbors as well as friends, Henry and Thomas enjoyed talking about inventions and ideas in their Florida hideaways. They had become so famous they

HENRY FORD

IIIIIIIIIIIIIIIIIIIIIIIIIIIIIIIIIIIIIII (1863–1947) IIIIIIIIIIIIIIIIIIIIIIIIIIIIIIIIIIIIIIIIIII

BORN THE ELDEST of six children on a farm in Michigan, Henry Ford grew up working on his father's farm machinery rather than in the fields or doing chores. At 16, he left home to work as an apprentice machinist and eventually landed a job with the Westinghouse company, working on steam-powered engines.

In 1891, when he was 28 years old, Ford went to work for the Edison Illuminating Company of Detroit as an engineer. He spent his spare time working on experiments with internal combustion engines, creating his own self-propelled vehicle, which he named the Quadricycle. He quit his job in 1899 and set up the Detroit Automobile Company with some investors, and began designing and building automobiles.

In 1903 Ford founded the Ford Motor Company. By 1908, production of his Model T automobile was booming. In 1913, he updated the factory to include moving assembly belts, which brought parts to the workers who stood in place to assemble vehicles. It was based on the moving belts his friend Thomas Edison used in the ore-crushing plant in New Jersey. The moving belts sped up production, and by 1918 half of all cars in America were Model Ts.

In 1914, Ford announced that he was giving his employees both shorter workdays and five dollars pay for a day's work. That doubled the employees' wages. Ford felt his success at selling cars depended on people being able to buy them. In 1926, Ford cut the workweek for his employees to five days, giving them both Saturday and Sunday off each week. It was the beginning of the five-day workweek in America.

Library of Congress, LC-USZ62-78374

Henry Ford also started a newspaper, created a history museum that was an entire village (Greenfield Village in Dearborn, Michigan), and promoted aviation. He died in 1947.

Thomas Edison loved fishing. When the pressure of inventing and producing got to be too much, Edison rented boats and took his employees on fishing trips in the water off Long Island. He fished like he experimented, however. Even when the fish weren't biting, he kept fishing, never willing to give up. On one trip he fished for two days without getting a bite, and the others had to make him quit so they could go home. At Seminole Lodge, Edison had a long pier built out into the Caloosahatchee River so boats could dock in the deeper channel out in the river. He often spent his days in Florida sitting on the pier with a fishing pole, thinking while waiting for a fish to bite. He caught mostly catfish. His wife said, "his greatest joy was catching a shark, which he would do occasionally." And, fishing was something he could do with his sons, who enjoyed it, too.

Experimenting with Plants

Plants fascinated Thomas Edison, who always searched for materials that could be useful in experiments. The bamboo filament had made his electric light bulb successful. Now in Florida, with its warm climate, he could work with exotic plants. His Florida laboratory, which was stuffed with machine tools, a steam

Florida State Archives

Edison with the Model T car Henry Ford gave to him. He kept it for years, even though Ford wanted to give him newer, improved models.

wanted to get away from newspaper reporters and visitors. Both men also wanted to study plant science and grow plants for experimental purposes.

engine, a dynamo, and electric motors, was painted green. The lab was a lot like the one in New Jersey, but smaller, of course. He could continue work he'd started up north while he was in Florida for the winter months. The nearby Caloosahatchee River was perfect for trying out new ideas with water. With the river so close, Edison could work on water sonar and equipment for boats while he was at Fort Myers.

Seminole Lodge provided lots of interesting raw material he couldn't find in New Jersey, such as Spanish moss, bamboo, palms, ocean sponges, and seashells. He also kept honeybees at Seminole Lodge, to pollinate the plants and to provide a source of beeswax for experiments.

In 1914, Edison, Ford, and Firestone traveled to an exhibit in San Francisco that showed off the use of electricity for cooking. The exhibit was called the "Electric Dinner," and the food was prepared on an electric stove. Afterward, the three went to visit Luther Burbank, who lived near Santa Rosa, California. Burbank was famous for his plant experiments. He crossbred thousands of plants to come up with new types, such as a spineless cactus he hoped would be good for cattle feed. Edison admired Burbank's work. "He is constantly busy creating new flowers and plants," Edison said. "This fellow knows

Florida State Archives

⬆ (ABOVE) Edison's chemistry laboratory at his Florida home. He kept up his experimenting here when the family came down from New Jersey during the winter months. ➔ (RIGHT) Henry Ford (left); Tien Lai Huang, the Chinese ambassador (center); and Thomas Edison. Edison's clothes are rumpled, as always.

that plants are not stagnant but can be changed to come up with new varieties of flowers with beautiful colors and forms."

Florida State Archives

Edison During World War I

Thomas Edison at a Navy base during World War I.

World War I broke out in Europe in 1914, and by 1917 the United States had entered the fighting. Edison was reluctant to support the war, but volunteered his services to the government. He was appointed to serve on the Naval Consulting Board, and he worked on developing underwater telephones, and detection devices for torpedoes and submarines. He created 42 marine warfare devices, including underwater sonar, a net to stop torpedoes, underwater searchlights, and night glasses.

Henry Ford was strongly against the United States entering a European war and argued for a diplomatic solution. As the nation was moving toward entering World War I, Ford rented a steamship and sent a large group of American peace activists to Europe to try to stop the war. As the ship pulled away from the pier in New York City, Ford begged his friend Edison to come along. Edison wanted diplomacy, not war, but he didn't go with Ford's group. The story goes that at the last minute, Henry Ford told Edison he'd pay him a million dollars to come along, but Edison didn't answer. Some think he simply didn't hear the offer, due to his deafness. Ford's "Peace Ship" didn't succeed, and the United States entered the war in 1917.

Greenfield Village

Henry Ford wanted to be sure ordinary people were remembered in history. He didn't like that history only remembered battles and political events. He built his own museum in Dearborn, Michigan, called Greenfield Village, where he brought in buildings from around the country to re-create scenes from days gone by. It was the country's first theme park attraction. It included a schoolhouse, a church, and stores. There were displays of all the tools and technology people had used in the past. But the most important feature was his friend Edison's laboratory. Ford always admired Edison, and he tried to re-create the same environment in which Edison had made his famous inventions. Ford hired workers to dismantle the aging and outdated laboratories at Menlo Park and Fort Myers and reassemble them for display in Michigan. They even scooped up soil from both locations to make the displays as accurate as possible.

When Greenfield Village opened to the public in 1929, Edison visited the lab display and told Ford, "Henry, it's 99.9 percent perfect." After all the effort to re-create the buildings, Ford worried something was wrong. "We never kept the old place this clean," Edison told him.

Mina Edison wasn't too thrilled that Henry Ford took her husband's old laboratory apart and moved it to Michigan. By the time Edison gave the 40-year-old building to Ford for his museum, the equipment was outdated and he no longer worked in it. But Mina didn't want to part with it. When Henry Ford's workers came over from next door and started dismantling the old building, she said, "I wish he would keep out of our backyard."

Edison's Final Project

In 1926, at the age of 80, Edison was ready to let his sons take over the business. Theodore and Charles had been working with him for years. Charles enjoyed the business side of things and was a manager, while Theodore enjoyed scientific experimentation and research. Charles ran the company, while Theodore focused on his own work. Edison had worried about Theodore, who was a talented mathematical physicist. Edison didn't like mathematics (maybe because he had never been very good at it), and he feared that if Theodore pursued mathematics, he would go to work for the physicist Albert Einstein instead of join the family company. But Edison needn't have worried. After Theodore's mother, Mina, died in 1947, Theodore gave half of his inheritance (in cash and company stock) to 2,700 employees of the Thomas A. Edison Industries.

Thomas Edison's sons from his first marriage, to Mary, were not included in running the company. Tom Jr., the eldest, tried various schemes to make money but was never successful. His father disowned him at one point, to protect himself from his son's creditors, but gave him a job with Edison Industries. Tom Jr. committed suicide five years after his father died. William, the second son, worried his father because he continually needed money to support various business schemes. He served in both the Spanish-American War and World War I and eventually moved to a country estate in New Jersey, supported by his father. When Thomas Edison died, he left very little to William in his will.

Though Edison's younger sons took over the business, Edison was not content to sit back and relax. Instead, he began to work as hard as he could to find a new source for rubber. This project, which was his last, was different from his others. It was nothing like motion pictures, telegraphs, phonographs, or electricity, which were ideas that connected with each other. Finding rubber in plants was entirely in nature, and had nothing to do with magnets and electricity. It was an idea that had challenged Thomas Edison for years, beginning in the 1880s when he first started testing vegetable plants for rubber content.

Rubber became important to the world with the age of the automobile. Rubber tires were an essential part of every vehicle. Rubber has always been in short supply because it is made from the sap of special trees that only grow in tropical locations. Rubber trees were tapped by cutting an opening in the trunk and draining out the sap, or latex, which was collected in buckets. Just like collecting maple syrup from maple trees, the tapped tree continued growing and could be tapped more than once. During the war, it had been very difficult to obtain rubber for tires, and Americans wanted a steady supply that could be made or grown at home. After the war, England controlled most of the world's rubber supply in the tropics and raised prices very high to help pay back war debts. High prices, limited supply—in the age

AMAZING RUBBER

RUBBER WAS FIRST discovered by the ancient Aztecs and Mayans of Central and South America. They made rubber balls for sporting games, and Mayans made a sort of rubber shoe by dipping their feet in the stuff. They even used rubber to make comfortable handles on farm tools. When Spanish explorers saw the bouncing balls, they were astounded—some thought it was magic or the work of evil spirits.

of automobiles and airplanes, it was essential to find a way to grow rubber in the United States. The federal government built a large experimental station in Florida to research plants for rubber. Henry Ford and Harvey Firestone tried growing rubber trees in Florida as well as Brazil and Africa. They urged their friend Edison to join them in searching for a solution.

Edison was 81 years old, and this new project brought a sparkle back into his eyes. He loved nothing better than a problem to solve. In no time, Thomas Edison was buried in plant research. "Everything has turned to rubber in our family," his wife said. "We talk rubber, think rubber, dream rubber. Mr. Edison refuses to let us do anything else." Edison said, "I've had 60 years in physics and mechanics, and now I have taken up something entirely different and it is mighty interesting and I am enjoying it."

He started by collecting all the plants he could find that had latex sap and pasting dried specimens on note cards. He figured that since his friend, Luther Burbank, could come up with new varieties of potatoes and flowers by crossbreeding plants, maybe he could do the same with plants that contained latex. He checked out more than 14,000 plants and tested many of them for sap content. He found 1,240 that had rubber content

and narrowed that list down to the 600 he thought might actually be easy to grow.

He soon focused on one plant, goldenrod. He experimented with growing the plant until he developed one type that grew over 12 feet (3.6 m) tall. Why goldenrod? "While many other plants had a somewhat higher content of rubber-producing juices," Edison said, "they were utterly impracticable as a growable and movable crop, and their manufacture would be far more complicated and expensive." Truly he had found a plant that would be as hardy as a weed across most of the nation. It could be grown quickly, which was better than waiting for trees to mature before tapping them.

His experiments showed he could obtain 12 percent natural rubber from goldenrod sap—something quite valuable. He developed a process to remove the latex from goldenrod plants. He obtained one of his last patents for his process of extracting rubber from plants.

What happened to Edison's idea of obtaining rubber from plants? At the same time, German chemists had already figured out how to make synthetic rubber from turpentine and acetylene, and American chemists soon followed their lead. In 1931, the DuPont Company patented neoprene, the first successful synthetic rubber. Two years later, Firestone was making automobile tires from

Laurie Carlson

Goldenrod is a native plant that grows wild in most of North America. It's now the state flower in Kentucky, Nebraska, and South Carolina. It has a yellow blossom and plume-like shape.

TEST A DANDELION FOR LATEX

LATEX is the plant sap that is used to produce natural rubber. Many plants contain latex. The common dandelion is one that's easy to examine.

YOU'LL NEED

* Bunch of dandelions
* Saucer
* Other plants for testing, such as milkweed, sagebrush, garden weeds

Break a dandelion stem in half and notice a milky white liquid slowly emerge. Squeeze drops of it onto the saucer, and see how much natural latex you can collect. Wait a few minutes for the water portion of the milky sap to evaporate, leaving only the latex. Scrape the latex off the saucer with your fingernail and roll it into a ball with your fingertips.

It's difficult to get much latex from dandelions, isn't it? Edison considered dandelions as a rubber source, and his friend Henry Ford researched using the plant as a source of latex to make rubber. Ford's experiments produced high-quality rubber from dandelions, but it was too difficult to grow them in large enough quantities to make much rubber.

What about other latex-producing plants? There are more than 400, including milkweed and sagebrush. Test some plants you find in your yard and see what you find. Researchers are still looking for the elusive new source for natural rubber.

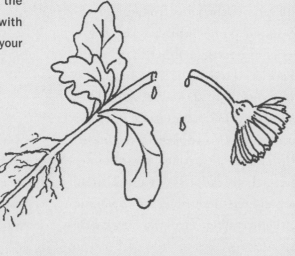

neoprene. Today about half the rubber we use is synthetic and half is from tapping rubber trees. The two types are often blended together to make a good product. Synthetic rubber, made from petroleum, isn't as flexible and can't take changes in temperature. Scientists are still trying to find another plant source for rubber that will grow in temperate climates, like in the United States.

Edison never intended to retire from his work. After turning over the management of the business to his son, he was free to work on the many ideas he hadn't gotten to yet. He left hundreds of designs, ideas, and projects unfinished. He simply ran out of time to work on them.

In one case, he tried to use solar energy. He knew solar flares affected the earth's magnetic force. He figured he could use a vein of magnetic iron ore in the earth to generate electrical charges if it was wrapped with a lot of wire to form an induction circuit. He put up two telephone poles on opposite sides of a hill that contained iron ore, then wound several miles of wire on the two poles. It didn't work, but he learned from it anyway.

Another project Edison took up was figuring out what he called "etheric force."

Etheric force was something he discovered very early in his career, and was ridiculed for, but could never explain. He worked on it from time to time for most of his adult life. In retrospect, it is one of his most important ideas. Edison knew some sort of sound waves moved through the air, but he couldn't control them. He experimented with sending messages up to equipment attached to flying kites, which would send the messages back to instruments on the ground, much like the way broadcasts are sent from earth to satellites

HEAT TEST A RUBBER BAND

WHAT'S SO SPECIAL about natural rubber, anyway? Why aren't man-made chemical materials just as good? Natural rubber has never been improved upon. It has the ability to contract, or shrink slightly, when heated. That's really important when making things like tires, which heat up from friction. If tires were pure synthetic rubber, they would stretch when heated and that would be a disaster! Even a rubber ball, with lots of vigorous bouncing, would lose its spring if it didn't contain natural latex rubber.

See for yourself with this experiment.

YOU'LL NEED

＊ Large rubber band
＊ A heavy object, like a hammer
＊ Hair dryer

Hang the rubber band from a doorknob, and then hang a hammer or another weight from the rubber band. It should stretch the band but not break it. Hold the hair dryer over the rubber band and turn it on. What happens? If the rubber band were made of synthetic materials, or other natural materials, it would stretch when warmed. But natural latex rubber doesn't do that. In fact, it does the opposite—it shrinks a bit when heated. The molecules in rubber become shorter as the rubber is heated, causing a stretched rubber band to contract. That ability to contract when heated makes it a perfect material for vehicle tires. No other material works as well for such things as airplane tires, which hit the landing surface at high speeds and get very hot.

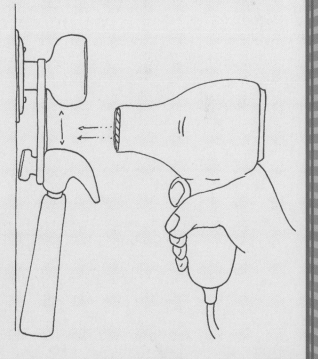

HOMEMADE FUNNY PUTTY

EXPERIMENTAL SCIENCE is full of happy accidents. One is still popular as a toy today. Silly Putty was an accidental invention. A researcher trying to make synthetic rubber accidentally dropped boric acid into silicone oil, creating the new putty. Scientists played around with the putty but couldn't find a use for it. Peter Hodgson bought the patent rights for $147 and began selling it as a children's toy. He packaged it in a plastic egg container because it was close to Easter. Silly Putty became very popular. When Hodgson died in 1976, his estate was worth $140 million.

YOU'LL NEED

* ½ cup (118 ml) Elmers' Glue-All or similar white glue
* Plastic container with lid
* ¼ cup (59 ml) liquid starch (found in the laundry section of the grocery store)
* Spoon

Pour the glue into the plastic container. Gradually pour the starch into the glue, and mix well. If the mixture is sticky, add more starch. When it gets thick enough to handle, begin kneading it with your hands on a kitchen counter, tabletop, or hard surface. Work it until it is smooth and glossy. Cover and refrigerate overnight. This putty can be cut with scissors, pulled, and twisted. Try some experiments of your own with the funny putty. Be sure to put it away for storage, however, as it can make a mess in carpet, fabric, and furniture if it dries.

and back to earth today. But Edison could never send telegraph messages using kites for a longer distance than three miles (4.8 km). If he had succeeded in figuring out how to control sound waves, he would have also invented wireless communications. As it was, his work paved the way for others to make those discoveries.

"Lights Out!"

In 1931, the nation was deep in financial depression. Thousands were jobless, the economy in shambles. Yet Edison, now 84, was still upbeat. His health was poor, and he was too weak to attend a lighting convention, so he sent a message, "My message to you is to be courageous. I have lived a long time. I have seen history repeat itself again and again. I have seen many 'depressions' in business. Always America has come out strong and more prosperous. Be as brave as your fathers were before you. Have faith—go forward." Though confined to a wheelchair much of the time, Edison still struggled to work in his laboratory in Florida. When he returned to New Jersey in the spring of 1931, he asked that everything from his laboratory be shipped to him. He knew he would never return to Seminole Lodge.

He died a few months later, from several disorders, including kidney failure and diabetes. To honor him and his contribution to the nation, President Hoover asked that all electric lights be turned off for one minute. On October 21 lights all across the country—even the torch on the Statue of Liberty—were turned off in his memory. The nation has never honored anyone else with such a tribute. What made it even more significant is that people couldn't keep the lights off for long—everyone had come to depend upon Edison's electrical inventions. The country simply couldn't do without electricity for more than a few minutes.

Late in his life, when reminded of all the inventions and topics he'd been involved in, Thomas Edison leaned back and said, "Say, I have been mixed up in a whole lot of things, haven't I?"

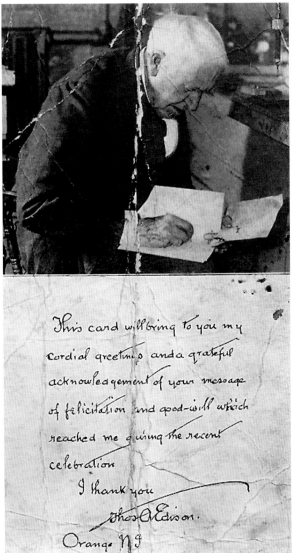

This card will bring to you my cordial greetings and a grateful acknowledgement of your message of felicitation and good-will which reached me during the recent celebration

I thank you

Thos A Edison.

Orange N.J.

Florida State Archives

Edison writing a card in 1929, two years before he died.

Florida State Archives

Thomas Edison died in 1931, at the age of 84. He was one of the most famous people in the world during his lifetime.

Resources

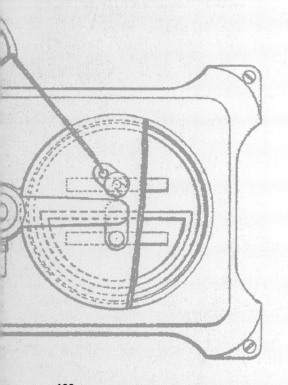

Thomas Edison's Major Inventions

1868	Vote Recorder	1879	Dynamo
1869	Printing Telegraph	1879	Incandescent Electric Light
1869	Stock Ticker	1881	Electric Motor
1872	Automatic Telegraph	1886	Talking Doll
1876	Electric Pen	1897	Moving Pictures Projector (Kinetoscope)
1877	Carbon Telephone Transmitter	1900	Storage Battery
1877	Phonograph		

Supply Sources

These companies carry hundreds of supplies useful for all kinds of science experiments, science fair exhibits, and interesting toys. Write or call for catalogs, or visit their Web sites.

Edmund Scientific
60 Pearce Avenue
Tonawanda, New York 14150
(800) 728-6999
www.scientificsonline.com

Science Stuff
7801 North Lamar Boulevard, Suite. E-190
Austin, Texas 78752-1016
(800) 795-7315
www.sciencestuff.com

PhysLink.Com
5318 East Second Street, #530
Long Beach, California 90803
(888) 438-9867
www.physlink.com

SK
777 East Park Drive
Tonawanda, New York 14150
(800) 828-7777
www.sciencekit.com

Places to Visit

Edison Birthplace Museum
9 Edison Drive
Milan, Ohio 44846
(419) 499-2135
www.tomedison.org
This is the house in which Thomas Edison was born. Today it's a small museum open to the public. Edison visited the house in 1923 and was shocked to see it was still lit with lamps and candles.

Thomas Edison House
729-31 E. Washington Street
Louisville, Kentucky
(502) 585-5247
Edison lived here after the Civil War, while he worked as a young telegrapher.

139

Edison Museum

Melissa Phillips, Director

350 Pine Street

Beaumont, Texas 77701

(409) 981-3089

www.edisonmuseum.org

Edison didn't live in Texas, but this museum is devoted to his life and work.

Edison National Historic Site

Main Street and Lakeside Avenue

West Orange, New Jersey 07052

(973) 736-2783

www.nps.gov/edis/home.htm

At this recently renovated site you can see the Edison family home and grounds, Glenmont, where Edison lived for 50 years. Visit Edison's laboratories, Thomas and Mina Edison's grave sites, and the film studio called Black Maria.

Edison Phonograph Museum

9812, rue Royale, Ste-Anne-de-Beaupré

Quebec, GOA 3CO Canada

www.phono.org/beaupre.html

This private museum is dedicated to collecting and exhibiting Edison's phonographs.

Edison Festival of Light

www.edisonfestival.org

Every February, people in Southwest Florida celebrate Edison's life with a nighttime parade and three-day festival in Fort Myers, Florida. Check the Internet site for exact events and dates.

Edison and Ford Winter Estates

2350 McGregor Boulevard

Fort Myers, Florida 33901

(239) 334-7419

www.Edison-ford-estate.com

You can visit the Florida winter homes of the Edison and Ford families—they were neighbors.

Thomas A. Edison Memorial Tower and Menlo Park Museum

37 Christie Street

Edison, New Jersey 08820

(732) 549-3299

www.edisonnj.org/menlopark/

This museum and tower was dedicated February 11, 1938, to commemorate Thomas Edison's 91st birthday. The tower marks the location of Edison's laboratory, and the museum contains some of Edison's inventions and products, as well as Edison memorabilia.

The Henry Ford Museum and Greenfield Village

Dearborn, Michigan

(313) 982-6100

(800) 835-5237

www.hfmgv.org

Here you can visit Thomas Edison's actual laboratory, which his friend, Henry Ford, painstakingly moved and preserved in the Greenfield Village living history museum. Ford's workers even moved some of the New Jersey soil surrounding the building, to make it more authentic!

National Museum of American History

Smithsonian Institution

14th Street and Constitution Avenue, N.W.

Washington, DC 20560

(202)633-1000

http://americanhistory.si.edu

The collections include several items related to Thomas Edison.

Port Huron Museum

Carnegie Center

1115 Sixth Street

Port Huron, Michigan

(810) 982-0891

www.phmuseum.org

This museum includes the Thomas Edison Depot Museum at the railroad depot built by the Grand Trunk Railway in 1858. Tour exhibits inside, then go outdoors to step into a restored baggage railcar which has been outfitted to re-create Thomas Edison's mobile chemistry laboratory and printing press.

Visitor Center—Electricity Museum

Rocky Reach Dam

Wenatchee, Washington

www.chelanpud.org

The museum, located inside a hydroelectric dam on the Columbia River, has a wonderful electricity exhibit, including some of Edison's experiments, equipment, and notebook pages.

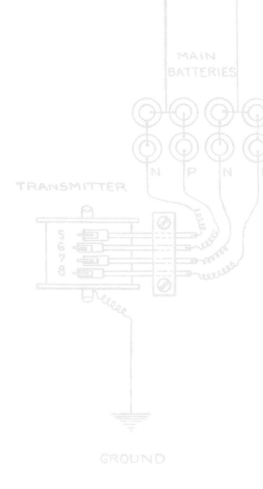

Web Sites to Explore

About Thomas Edison

www.minot.k12.nd.us/mps/edison/aboutte.html

This site is operated by Edison Elementary School, in Minot, North Dakota. It has a lot of information and links to other Edison-related sites.

Early Recorded Sounds

www.tinfoil.com

This site provides information about early methods of recording sounds and has photographs and audio excerpts from music first recorded on wax cylinders.

Thomas A. Edison Papers
Rutgers University
http://edison.rutgers.edu/
The collection is enormous, and many of Edison's papers and documents are available online at this Web site.

Edison's Home Page
www.thomasedison.com
Gerald Beals operates this private Web site that is full of information and images of Thomas Edison.

Thomas Edison's Inventions in the 1900s and Today: From New to You
National Endowment for the Humanities
http://edsitement.neh.gov/view_lesson_plan.asp
  ?id=408
This site explores and explains technology, in both Edison's day and the present.

Electrical Safety World
www.progress-energy.com/shared/esw/links
This site focuses on electricity and includes information about Thomas Edison and other inventors as well as electrical safety information.

Edison After Forty
http://americanhistory.si.edu/Edison/

This Web exhibit by the Smithsonian Institution includes several different collections of images, showing Edison's life and his inventions.

Edisonian Museum
http://www.edisonian.com
This inventor's Web site focuses on early Edisonian electric artifacts.

History of Telegraphy
http://collections.ic.gc.ca/cable/htelegr.htm
This Canadian government Web site has detailed information about laying the undersea telegraph cable between Newfoundland and Ireland, replacing earlier plans to use steamboats and carrier pigeons to send messages across the Atlantic Ocean.

Institute of Electrical and Electronics Engineers (IEEE) Virtual Museum
www.ieee-virtual-museum.org/index.php
Designed for students aged 10–18, educators, and the general public, the goal of this site is to "enhance understanding of the principles of electrical and information sciences and technologies within a historical context."

New York Public Library Digital Gallery
http://digitalgallery.nypl.org

You can find dozens of photographs of Thomas Edison by entering his name in the Search portal.

The Spanish-American War in Motion Pictures

http://memory.loc.gov/ammem/sawhtml/saw
  home.html

You can watch some of the actual films made by the Edison Manufacturing Company that have been preserved in the Library of Congress's American Memory collection.

U.S. Patent Office

www.uspto.gov/go/kids

This fun Web site has invention games and activities for kids.

Bibliography

(Books noted by ✳ are suitable for kids ages nine and older.)

✳ Adair, Gene. *Thomas Alva Edison: Inventing the Electric Age.* New York: Oxford University Press, 1996.

Baldwin, Neil. *Edison: Inventing the Century.* New York: Hyperion, 1995.

Clark, Ronald W. *Edison: The Man Who Made the Future.* New York: G. P. Putnam's Sons, 1977.

✳ Delano, Marfe Ferguson. *Inventing the Future: A Photobiography of Thomas Alva Edison.* Washington, DC: National Geographic Society, 2002.

Dyer, Frank Lewis, and Thomas Commerford Martin. *Edison: His Life and Inventions.* New York: Harper Brothers, 1910.

✳ *Edison Etc.* Salt Lake City, UT: The Wild Goose Company, 1994.

Edison Portland Cement Company. *The Romance of Cement.* Boston: Edison Portland Cement Co., 1926.

Essig, Mark. *Edison and the Electric Chair.* New York: Walker & Company, 2003.

Flatow, Ira. *They All Laughed: From Light Bulbs to Lasers, the Fascinating Stories Behind the Great Inventions That Have*

Changed Our Lives. New York: Harper-Perennial, 1993.

Frost, Lawrence A. *The Edison Album: A Pictorial Biography of Thomas Alva Edison.* Seattle, WA: Superior Publishing Co., 1969.

✳ Guthridge, Sue. *Thomas A. Edison: Young Inventor.* New York: Aladdin Paperbacks, 1959.

Israel, Paul. *Edison: A Life of Invention.* New York: John Wiley, 1998.

Jenkins, Reese V., et al. *The Papers of Thomas A. Edison.* 4 vols. Baltimore, MD: The Johns Hopkins University Press, 1989.

Jonnes, Jill. *Empires of Light: Edison, Tesla, Westinghouse, and the Race to Electrify the World.* New York: Random House, 2003.

Josephson, Matthew. *Edison: A Biography.* New York: History Book Club, 2003; reprint of McGraw Hill, 1959.

Owen, David. "Concrete Jungle." *The New Yorker,* November 10, 2003, 62–66.

✳ Sullivan, George. *Thomas Edison.* Scholastic Inc., 2001.

✳ The Thomas Alva Edison Foundation. *The Thomas Edison Book of Easy and Incredible Experiments.* New York: John Wiley & Sons, 1988.

Thulesius, Olav. *Edison in Florida: The Green Laboratory.* Gainesville, FL: University Press of Florida, 1997.

Vanderbilt, Byron. *Thomas Edison, Chemist.* Washington, DC: American Chemical Society, 1971.

Wachhorst, Wyn. *Thomas Alva Edison: An American Myth.* Cambridge, MA: The Massachusetts Institute of Technology Press, 1981.

✳ Zemlicka, Shannon. *Thomas Edison.* New York: Barnes & Noble Books, 2004.

Index

Also available from Chicago Review Press

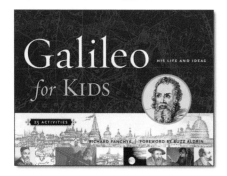

Galileo for Kids

His Life and Ideas
25 Activities
By Richard Panchyk, Foreword by Buzz Aldrin

Galileo, one of history's best-known scientists, is introduced in this illuminating activity book. Children will learn how Galileo's revolutionary discoveries and sometimes controversial theories changed our world and laid the groundwork for modern astronomy and physics. Activities include playing with gravity and motion, making a pendulum, observing the moon, and painting with light and shadow.

Ages 9 & up
Two-color illustrations throughout
$16.95 (CAN $22.95) 1-55652-566-4

Leonardo da Vinci for Kids

His Life and Ideas
21 Activities
By Janis Herbert

"One of a series of terrific history-based activity books."　　　—*Home Education Magazine*

The marriage of art and science is celebrated in this beautifully illustrated biography and activity book. Kids will begin to understand the important discoveries that da Vinci made through inspiring activities such as determining the launch angle of a catapult, sketching birds and other animals, and learning to look at a painting.

Ages 8 & up
Four-color illustrations throughout
$16.95 (CAN $22.95) 1-55652-298-3

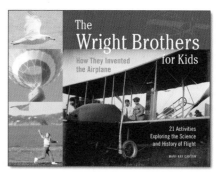

The Wright Brothers for Kids

How They Invented the Airplane
21 Activities Exploring the Science and History of Flight
By Mary Kay Carson

"This book is one of the best I have ever found about the Wright brothers and the invention of human flight."　　　—*KLIATT*

At a time when most people still hadn't ridden in an automobile, Wilbur and Orville Wright built the first powered, heavier-than-air flying machine. Woven throughout the heartwarming story of the two brothers are activities that highlight their ingenuity and problem-solving abilities. Activities include making a Chinese flying top, building a kite, bird watching, and designing a paper glider.

Ages 9 & up
Two-color illustrations throughout
$14.95 (CAN $20.95) 1-55652-477-3

CHICAGO REVIEW PRESS

Distributed by
Independent Publishers Group
www.ipgbook.com

www.chicagoreviewpress.com

Available at your favorite bookstore or by calling (800) 888-4741